the Girl Guide Annual 1983

edited by Penny Morris

THIS ANNUAL BELONGS TO...

£2.75

Cutting the ICE

by Penny Morris

photographs by Derek Bayes

Looking at the photographs on these pages you'd probably think the beautiful sculptures are made of glass, or even plastic. That's what most people think when they first see an ice sculpture. I recently visited the man who made them, and I was amazed at his skill. His name is Duncan Hamilton and he lives in Putney.

Duncan has been carving ice for about eight years. Originally he worked as a chef and teacher of professional cookery, occasionally making an ice carving for a banquet or display. His reputation as an ice sculptor grew, and Duncan gave up his teaching job and is now the only freelance ice sculptor working in the United Kingdom.

The ice that Duncan uses is very specific. It comes from Lowestoft, where it is made by a firm which makes fish ice. It is brought from Lowestoft by lorry in blocks, each weighing 3cwt. The mould in which the ice is made holds 35 gallons of water and each block takes three days to freeze! The blocks are made in a particular way so that the ice is clear and very stable, and will not melt too quickly.

During the winter Duncan makes about six sculptures a week, but in the summer there is very little demand. Most of the sculptures are commissioned by hotels, but Duncan also makes sculptures for parties and important business occasions. Some sculptures require more than one block of ice: Duncan told me about a model of the Golden Gate Bridge which took five blocks of ice and was twelve feet long!

The tools which Duncan uses are very special. They come from Japan and you need a licence to buy them. They are made from Samurai steel, which is very hard, and each tool is made by one man and bears his name engraved upon it. Ice sculpture is very popular in Japan—most hotels employ a full-time sculptor. When Duncan first started to carve ice he used carpenter's tools; having a set of proper ice-carving tools made a great difference to his work, as he can now carve with greater accuracy and precision.

The actual sculpting is done in the open air, as Duncan prefers to work

The block of ice is marked out with the shape of an eagle

Duncan starts by cutting out the basic outline

A magnificent eagle ready for display. It will take about six hours to melt

The eagle begins to take shape

These sacks of snow...

replied that for him that was part of the attraction of working in ice—each sculpture is unique and makes an impact because you know it won't be there tomorrow. I asked whether people realised the sculptures were carved out of ice. Duncan said most people thought they were glass and did not believe they were ice until they touched them. The sculptures are always made from clear ice, but

...become this lovely Snoopy sculpture

outside. He shares a warehouse in Battersea with several ice suppliers and usually works in the yard there. He has to dress warmly when working, usually wearing a ski suit and heavy boots. Duncan has numerous pairs of gloves—if he is doing a demonstration he will wear a fairly thin, smart pair of golfing gloves, but when he is working alone he wears thick industrial-style gloves.

I asked Duncan how he transports the finished sculptures, expecting him to say he used a small van. "Oh, no," he said. "I wrap them in a duvet and put them in the back of the car!"

The work of ice sculpting is very hard. Duncan can only carve for

Another magnificent bird sculpture

by using clever lighting it is possible to make the sculpture look a particular colour.

Duncan doesn't sculpt snow commercially, but he does sometimes do snow-sculpture demonstrations. The snow for the Snoopy sculpture was brought in sacks from Billingsgate Market, where there is an ice crusher which breaks up the fish ice. Snoopy was made for a group of children in a park one day. Next time it snows, why don't you try and make a special shape—a snow dog or cat, or even a snowy owl!

about two hours at a time as it is very tiring. He must also spend several days working out designs and plans for the sculpture so that he knows exactly what he is going to do before he begins. He marks the outline of the design on two faces of the ice block and only then begins to carve. The eagle in the photographs took about an hour and a half and is one of Duncan's favourite carvings. The swan takes only about 35 minutes to make and is very popular.

I wondered whether Duncan minded that his masterpieces disappeared within a matter of hours. He

The swan is one of the most popular sculptures

This was made for a party

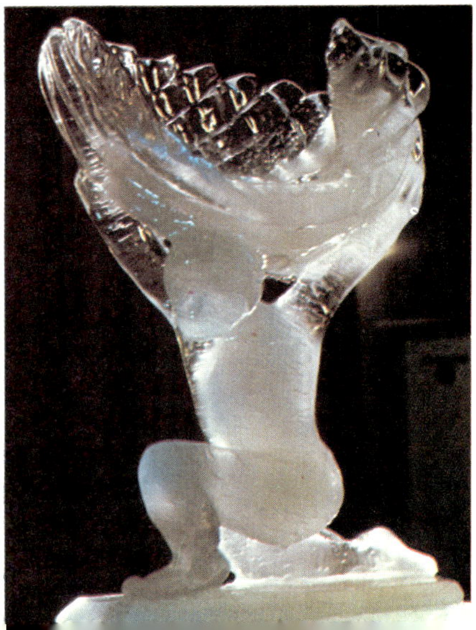

A GIFT FOR GUINEVERE

by Susan Cooper

illustrated by Alexa Rutherford

Summer had come to Camelot. Bright flags fluttered from every tower, and the whole town was buzzing with excitement for, after many long months away, King Arthur was coming home. A tournament was to be held in his honour the next day and everyone in the town smiled cheerfully as they went about their business—except one girl.

Lynette, Sir Kay's youngest daughter, came running out of the castle and down the meadow, her chestnut plaits flying behind her and her long blue skirt held high. Frolly, her little dog, trotted anxiously beside her, wondering why his mistress should have such an angry face on such a bright morning.

A slim dark girl was coming up the hill, carrying a basket of roses. Hearing the footsteps, she looked up in surprise. "Why, what is wrong, Lynette?" she asked.

"Oh, Jenny, everything's all wrong. I am in sad disgrace. Mother has just told me that I am not to make the presentation to Queen Guinevere tonight after all. Eloise is to do it instead."

This was terrible news. Lynette had been looking forward to the presentation since long before Easter, and had practised her speech almost every day.

"Eloise?" said Jenny in surprise. "Poor Eloise. She is far too timid to do it properly."

"Poor Eloise!" stormed Lynette. "Poor little good, sly, sneaky Eloise who never answers back!"

"But why did your mother change her mind?"

"I broke two needles when we were sewing this morning, then I stitched my work onto the knee of my gown, and pricked my finger, dropping blood on the white linen . . . but what finished it all, Mother says, was that I let Frolly run off with Eloise's handkerchief and hide it somewhere. We couldn't find it again."

"Never mind," said Jenny soothingly. "I expect your mother will relent. She usually does!"

"Not this time," replied Lynette ruefully. "Eloise's mother was there and she heard her say it."

Jenny linked arms with her friend and gave her hand a little squeeze. "I must take these flowers to the castle. Come back with me and try to pretend you do not care. Let us think about something else instead . . . perhaps your brother Rohan will win first prize at the tournament tomorrow!"

Lynette was not consoled. "In the last tournament," she said scornfully, "Rohan jammed his helmet down upon his head as a joke and then could not pull it off again when it was time to collect his prize—he spent an hour with the blacksmith for his foolishness, having it removed."

By this time the girls had entered the castle courtyard. They climbed up a flight of stone steps to the morning room, where a group of young girls sat weaving garlands. It was a large, square room, with one wall completely covered by a magnificent tapestry depicting knights in battle. On the opposite wall, on a high shelf, lay a delicate rose-coloured velvet cushion, on top of which rested an embroidered golden bag with a silken drawstring and tassle. Jenny looked up at the bag with interest, but Lynette turned her head away, for inside it, she knew, was the jewel-encrusted mirror which was to be presented to the Queen.

Jenny set down her basket. "I came to ask if I could help with the garlands," she said.

A small, pale girl looked up. "We need more help, else we will not be done in time," she said shyly. Her voice was scarcely more than a whisper, but it seemed to Lynette that it held reproach. This irked her.

"Shouldn't you be practising your speech, Eloise, so that you make no mistakes?" she asked blandly.

One of the girls smothered a laugh. "It will not matter," she remarked, "for no one will be able to hear what Eloise is saying anyway."

"Hush, Alice," murmured Jenny. She glanced uneasily across the room. Eloise went on threading the flowers together as if she had not heard, but two red patches appeared on her white cheeks.

Alice made a face at Jenny and tossed her head. "I don't see why I should not speak out," she continued. "We all teased Lynette about the presentation, we said she'd be sure to drop the gift, or trip over her gown... she laughed as much as we did! But nobody must say anything to Eloise. They only chose her because there was no one else; Jenny and I will be dancing and the others are too young."

Jenny began to be afraid that there might be trouble. Eloise, though quiet, was given to sudden fits of temper when roused. Then Frolly saved the situation. Tired of sitting still, he began to scamper around the room. The tapestry seemed to fascinate him particularly, for he scrabbled at it with his paws and thrust his nose beneath the hem.

"Do you think he has hidden a bone there?" asked Alice.

Jenny, who was the nearest, went to look. "Nothing at all. Not even a spider," she announced. As she was speaking, the door opened and an elderly maidservant came in.

"My Lady Emilia says that the King's procession is in sight and you may go to the wall above the Great Gate to view it," she told them.

They needed no second bidding. Like a flock of bright birds in their gaily coloured dresses they sped out of the room and up the winding staircase to the battlements. Lynette led the way and Eloise, insisting on tidying up before she left, was last. Martha, the maidservant, locked the door behind them.

Above the gateway, the girls stood on tiptoe, peering over the high parapet.

Slowly the great procession wound its way towards the castle. A hundred foot soldiers came first, marching in lines of four, their spears glittering in the sunshine; then rank upon rank of knights in shining armour, mounted on splendid steeds. At their head rode the King, straight and tall upon his magnificent bay horse, with Queen Guinevere beside him, radiantly beautiful upon a snow white palfrey. The girls gazed down, entranced.

The watchers lingered until the last baggage mule had trotted sedately into the courtyard; then, with slippered feet pattering lightly on the flagstones, they made their way back to the morning room.

When they reached the door they had to wait. Old Martha, flustered, was peering shortsightedly on the floor around her. A tall youth, with fair hair and a helpful smile, was leaning against the wall and offering advice.

"Alas, young ladies," panted Martha, "I have dropped the key and cannot see where it has fallen."

"And what is Rohan doing here?" enquired Lynette crisply.

"I am telling Martha the likeliest places to look, of course," he replied.

"The likeliest place to find it," his sister said, giving him a push, "is underneath your foot. Shame on you to tease poor Martha so," she added, as the key revealed itself beneath his long pointed shoe.

Rohan laughed, unabashed, and strolled away.

"Come on," said Jenny, "we must finish the garlands."

"What Eloise should be doing," said Alice mischievously, "is practising her speech."

Eloise lifted pink-rimmed eyes. "I—I do not wish to," she muttered.

"It would be better if you did," Lynette told her frankly. "I know... let's do it properly... I'll be Queen Guinevere and you can present me with the mirror, Eloise... I'll go and get it." She climbed up onto a small table to reach the shelf. They all watched anxiously: except Eloise, who continued to weave her garland with shaking fingers, and Frolly, who was trying to catch his tail.

Suddenly Lynette gave a great cry and almost fell off the stool. "It has gone!" she gasped in horror. "The mirror has gone—the bag is empty!"

"Sorcery!" cried Alice at once.

"Not sorcery, but theft!" Lynette climbed slowly down, holding the empty bag in her hand.

"But who would do such a thing?" Jenny was appalled. "This is worse than theft. It is an insult to the Queen. Even if it were but taken in jest..."

"Rohan!" Lynette broke in angrily. "Only Rohan would dare to do such a thing... and he was here but a moment ago. When my father hears of this, Rohan will be sent away from Camelot."

She rushed out of the room, with Alice at her heels.

Soon they were back, pulling Rohan along like a prisoner between them.

"What game is this?" he asked, smiling indulgently.

"No game... the Queen's mirror is gone. We demand that you return it."

Jenny saw the smile go from his lips, the colour drain from his face.

"I swear that I know nothing of this," he protested.

"Indeed!" answered Lynette scornfully. "In the same way that you knew nothing of Martha's key. When my father hears of this, you will be sent away at once."

"No more tournaments to win," thought Jenny sadly, "no chance of knighthood now." Then suddenly, she remembered the incident with the key. "It couldn't have been Rohan!" she exclaimed. "When Martha dropped her key, the door was still locked."

In the silence that followed, the young squire drew a shaky breath.

"Thank you, Jenny," he said gruffly, "I am grieved to think that the others believed I would do such a thing." Then he straightened his shoulders. "We still have to find the mirror," he said crisply. "It would be best to begin by searching this room."

They hunted high and low, beneath the table, under the benches, in the closets, behind the shutters of the high windows, and even in Lady Emilia's own casket, but they found nothing. Then, just as she was about to give up in despair, Jenny remembered something she had noticed when Frolly was scrabbling around at the tapestry. Kneeling down beside it, she lifted the hem and found a place where the stitches had given way. Carefully she felt along it with her fingers and there, concealed within the hem as in a pocket, she found the precious mirror.

"Jenny has found the mirror!" Alice called out excitedly.

She began to dance with joy, but Lynette looked grave. "Why—it must have been one of *us* who hid it," she said unhappily.

"I don't believe that for a moment!" Alice said, shocked, but even as she spoke, a cry from the corner made them turn round in alarm, just in time to see Eloise fall to the floor in a crumpled heap. She had fainted.

"I'll go and get Martha or Lady Emilia," said Rohan and hurried out of the room.

Jenny took Eloise's cold hands and began to rub them. As she did so, the girl opened her eyes and caught Jenny tightly by the wrist. "Don't tell my mother," she implored.

"Tell her what?" inquired Lynette, puzzled.

"Please don't tell her that I hid the mirror." Her voice was so low that they had to strain to hear her. "I found the hole in the tapestry when I was looking for my handkerchief... it gave me an idea... I meant no insult to the Queen... nor to hurt Rohan. I just thought that if the mirror were lost, I shouldn't have to make the speech. Oh, Jenny, I was so frightened!"

"But why not simply say that you didn't want to do it?" asked Lynette.

"Mother would have been so angry. Oh, Jenny, what can I do?"

Jenny smiled gently. "Have no fear," she said reassuringly. "We will see that it all comes right."

Later, when Rohan had returned with Lady Emilia, Jenny spoke simply and with perfect truth.

"Eloise will not be well enough to make the presentation," she said.

Surprisingly, Lady Emilia looked relieved. "Then, in spite of her behaviour, Lynette will have to do it after all," she replied.

When she had gone, taking Eloise with her, Rohan spoke out. "This story must go no further," he told them. "It would grieve the Queen if anything of this should reach her ears."

They agreed fervently and Lynette spoke up for them all. "If we had been kinder to Eloise, this would never have happened," she said. "None of us realised how she was feeling... none, that is, except Jenny."

That evening, everyone gathered in the Great Hall. On the raised golden throne sat King Arthur, with his beautiful Queen beside him, surrounded by the bravest knights and the fairest ladies in the land.

Eloise had recovered enough to watch the proceedings and sat quietly with her mother, thankful to escape all notice.

Rohan, standing proudly with the other young squires, dreamed of the great deeds he would perform when he had proved that he was no longer an idle prankster... and of the slim dark girl he hoped one day to be worthy of.

Jenny herself, as yet unaware of Rohan's thoughts, stood with the other girls holding their garlands, waiting to dance before their majesties.

Then a single trumpet sounded and all eyes turned towards the back of the hall. Slowly, Lynette walked down the length of the room, carrying the precious mirror on its velvet cushion. Making a perfect curtsey, she offered the gift to Queen Guinevere and made her speech clearly and without mistake.

When the Queen had thanked Lynette, King Arthur called for music and the minstrels struck up a merry tune. The girls stepped forward and the dance began.

Unnoticed by anyone, two bright eyes peered out from under a curtain at the back of the hall. Frolly looked round anxiously for his mistress and then, seeing her smiling face, wagged his tail enthusiastically. If Lynette was happy, then so was he!

The story of the SILVER FISH

by Tin Forbes illustrated by Chris Sheridan

Nowadays the Silver Fish is 'the highest award for exceptionally good service to the Guide Movement as a whole, in more than one capacity and usually for more than one country'.

But it was not always an award, nor was it shaped like a sardine as it is today. In 1910, which, as you know, was the beginning of Guiding, there was an 'Order of the Silver Fish' which Guides and Guiders could win if they passed nineteen interest badges—in those days called efficiency badges. In fact there were only two efficiency badges at that time which you did *not* need for the Silver Fish—Signaller and Sailor.

In 1912, in the first Guide handbook, we read that the Order of the Silver Fish is either presented as a reward for winning many badges, or for very special distinction. Why a fish? It was chosen because 'the fish is the emblem of one who has, by dint of hard study and determination, mastered so many difficulties that she is able to swim against the stream of trouble in life', to quote the *Girl Guides Gazette* of October 1915.

In 1916 the first Canadian Girl Guide received the Silver Fish. Of course, the Commonwealth countries have their own special awards, but the Silver Fish is one which we have in common. These countries wanted the Silver Fish to be a link within the Commonwealth, so it is only awarded by Commonwealth Headquarters in London upon the recommendation of a country's national headquarters. In all, 14 Silver Fishes were gained by Guides in 1916 for exceptional efficiency and good work, but it was not long before the question of qualifying for the Silver Fish was under consideration.

old.... **....and new**

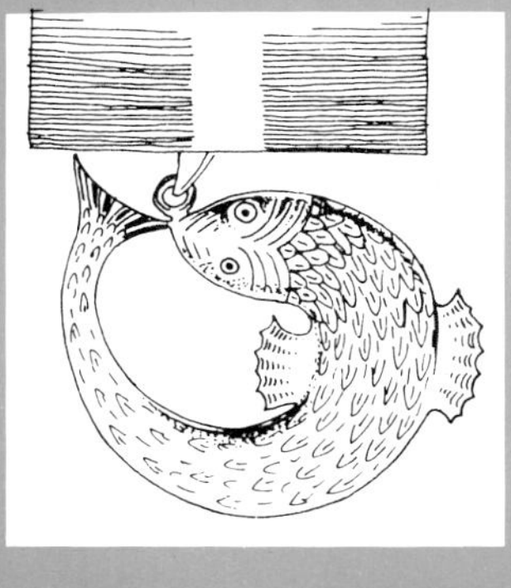

In 1918 we read that 'the Silver Fish is only awarded from Headquarters on the recommendation of the County Commissioner for some very special service to the Movement. Application to be made without the knowledge of the recipient'. Naturally a new design was thought to be necessary for the new kind of Silver Fish, and do you know who agreed to do this? Robert Baden-Powell, our Founder and the husband of the World Chief Guide. However, all those Guides who were in the middle of working for the earlier kind of Silver Fish award were allowed to complete the necessary qualifications. The last old style Silver Fish was awarded in 1920.

Gradually, over the years, the wording for the Silver Fish Award changed, until it became what it is today. Because it is now the very highest award for good service in the Guide Movement, very few Silver Fish are awarded. In 1980 there were only two, so you can see how exceptional they are.

How would you like to have been called Guide Anybody (Silverfished)? Yes, it's true, that really was put after the name of a Guide who had won the 'Order of the Silver Fish'!

GET WEAVING!

by Shireen Bonner

illustrated by Chris Sheridan

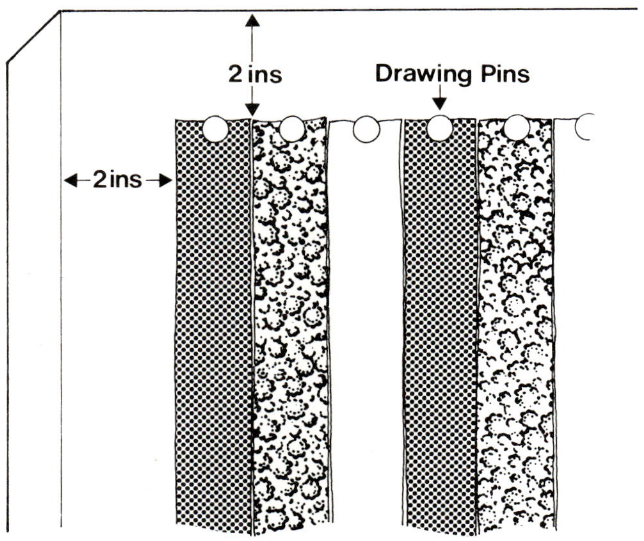

Handweaving is one of the most ancient arts, and it is enjoying a great revival of interest as more and more people rediscover traditional crafts. While most woven fabrics nowadays are machine made, the satisfaction derived from creating your own fabric is enormous. You can experiment with colour, yarns and textures, old strips of cloth can be made into colourful 'rag rugs', and even string can be used to great effect. Weaving can achieve stunning results—whether you weave on a sophisticated floor loom or improvise with a clothes horse.

Most people have done *some* weaving, perhaps without realising it. Anyone who has darned a sock has woven, for setting up threads which run in one direction (the ***warp***) and passing another thread over and under them (the ***weft***) is the basis of all weaving. This repeated 'over-under' motion is commonly known as ***tabby*** weave.

It is far easier to weave if the warp remains at a constant tension, and providing tension is the primary function of a ***loom.*** A loom can be anything from a massive industrial machine to a simple picture frame: anything which will hold pieces of yarn taut. Some beautiful pieces of weaving have been created on looms no more complicated than warp threads being weighted by stones.

Another simple loom is the back strap. The pressure of the body against a strap worn around the back controls the tension of the weaving being done in front. Many weavers in parts of Indonesia and Central America use this method.

With the exception of belt and tapestry weaving, most fabrics are woven on floor and table looms. The advantage of these looms is that they have mechanisms for lifting every other thread (or series of threads, depending on how the loom is ***warped up***) controlled by foot pedals on a floor loom, and by levers on a table loom. Each time a pedal or lever is worked, the desired warp threads (in tabby weave, each alternate one) are made to rise and, in some cases, to lower, too. This creates a space between the warp threads, known as a ***shed***, through which the weft, contained in a ***shuttle***, is then passed. A shuttle is a streamlined tool that moves swiftly and smoothly through the shed, avoiding any messy tangles with the warp threads!

The pedal or lever is then released and the warp threads return to their 'flat' position, ready for another row of weaving.

To keep the weaving neat and uniform, it helps if the weft is 'beaten' tightly into the rest of the weaving before continuing with the next row. This is done with a beater which swings back and forth to 'beat' the cloth. On simpler looms, a stick can be used as a beater, but one is already built into a floor or table loom. Another feature of the floor and table loom is that it can be prepared—warped up—to weave specific patterns and designs, as well as plain tabby weave.

Two striking examples of plain or tabby weaving are tartan plaids used for kilts, scarves, etc, and Madras cotton from India. Here the pattern is achieved by warping up the loom so that certain colours of the warp are in sequence, and likewise using certain colours of weft yarn in a specific order.

Two examples of simple ***pattern*** weaving are tweeds and herringbones. Here the actual ***weave***, not just the colours, create the pattern. Depending on the sophistication of the loom, handweavers are able to produce the most spectacular and ornate patterns, like exotic Chinese and Persian brocades, and woven Kashmiri shawls from India.

These are just a few of the many

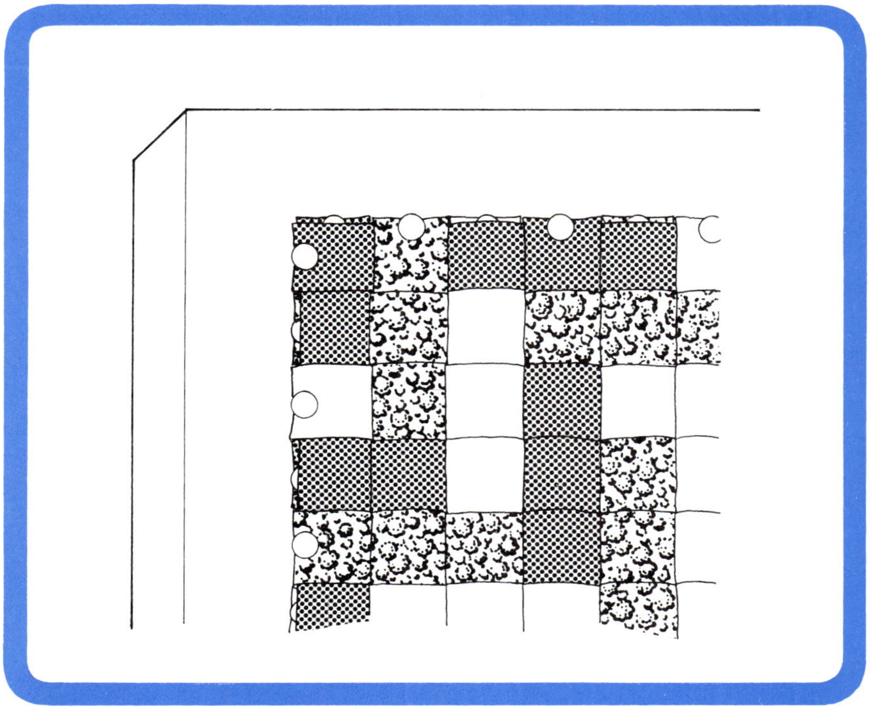

kinds of weaving throughout the world. However, it is possible to create beautiful textiles without any elaborate equipment. Some beautiful weaving is worked on a simple frame loom, which can be easily and cheaply constructed at home. Frame-loom weaving is a perfect introduction to the craft as it can serve as a 'sampler' for experimenting with techniques and colour. Looms of this type are used for tapestry weaving and, depending on size, some kinds of rug weaving. With tapestry weaving, the warp is completely covered by the weft, which alone creates the design. In most other forms of weaving, the warp is an integral part of the pattern.

Why not try this simple cushion project in very basic handweaving? It can be done with the minimum amount of preparation and equipment.

Once you try weaving, don't be surprised if you never want to stop, for the sense of achievement on completing a project is enormous! When you have mastered the basic techniques you may want to experiment and move on to more complex weaving. Don't be disheartened if you have difficulties with your first project. Like anything else, practice makes perfect, and once you understand the basics of weaving, nothing will hold you back!

If you are interested in learning weaving in a class, enquire about evening or weekend classes in your area. If there are no classes near you, visit the textile department of your nearest school or college, and see if a teacher or student would be willing to start one if enough Guides in your Company are interested. There are many informative books on handweaving, and for a real treat, visit a science museum and see some of the looms on show.

you need:

piece of 50cm square plywood board, 1.25cm thick.
36 45cm strips of coloured cotton or other non-fraying fabric, 2.5cm wide, (12 strips in bold print, 12 in small print, 12 in a plain complementary colour)
45cm square piece of cotton or other strong material for backing the weaving
45cm square piece of coloured velvet, or thick cotton, for the back of the cushion cover
36 drawing pins
pencil and ruler
tacking thread
cotton the same colour as the 'back' of the cover
large needle
fasteners, eg press-studs

Draw a line 45cm long 5cm away from two opposite ends of the board. Pin down 18 strips of cotton at the top and bottom of the board so that the ends touch the lines you have drawn. Pin at the very ends of the strips. Alternate the strips in series of three—bold print, small print, plain etc. This forms the ***warp***.

Using strips in the same sequence as the warp, weave the remaining 18 strips over and under the warp. Pass each strip of ***weft*** through one at a time, ensuring that it is pulled neatly to the ends, and lies flat. As you weave each strip, pin the weft in place at the sides if this helps to hold it down.

When you have completed the weaving, unpin it very carefully, making sure it all stays in place. Turn the weaving over so that the wrong side is facing up. Place the strong cotton over the wrong side and pin the two pieces together around the edges. Tack, then using a neat back stitch or a sewing machine, sew along all four sides leaving at least .60cm seam.

Pin together the velvet or the backing fabric and the weaving with their ***right*** sides facing, pinning only three sides. Tack, then sew with a neat back stitch or machine stitch leaving .60cm seam. One side is left open.

Turn cushion cover inside out, pushing the corners out with the wrong end of a knitting needle and neatly hem the edges that have been left open. Fix three press-studs along the opening to fasten the cover once the cushion is inside. Finally, iron the cover carefully.

PUZZLE PAGE

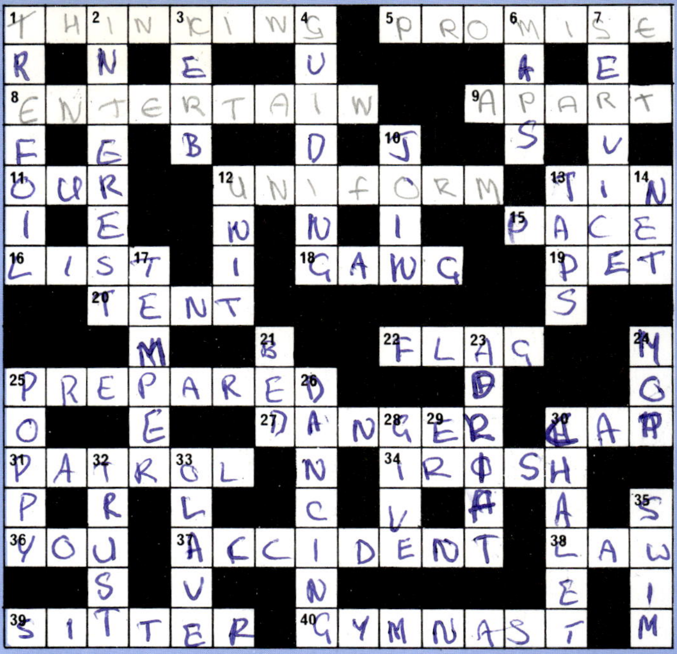

GUIDING CROSSWORD

by Penny Morris

ACROSS

1 What all Guides should be doing on February 22nd (8)
5 You make this when you are enrolled (7)
8 Do this to gain an Interest Badge with a mask on it (9)
9 In camp, keep wet and dry clothes..... (5)
11 and 30 down Guide Home in Adelboden, Switzerland (3 & 6)
12 Guides are proud to wear this (7)
13 Useful metal for camp crockery! (3)
15 Twenty running, twenty walking is Scout's.... (4)
16 Check off your kit on this before going to camp (4)
18 The show started by Ralph Reader for Scouts and Guides (4)
19 Look after one of these for Friend to Animals Badge (3)
20 Protects you from the rain when camping! (4)
22 Guides learn to hoist this, and keep it flying (4)
25 Guides should always BE this! (8)
27 It is safest to try and avoid this (6)
30 Top of your uniform (3)
31 You will be a member of one of these when you join a Company (6)
34 March 17th is a special day for these Guides (5)
36 Not me! (3)
37 Learn to prevent one and gain a badge towards the Service Emblem (8)
38 Important part of the Promise, which every Guide tries to keep (3)
39 Use one of these if the grass is damp at camp (6)
40 Interest badge requiring floor and apparatus work (7)

DOWN

1 Small three-leafed plant taken for the Association's badge (7)
2 These badges are sewn on the right sleeve of your uniform (8)
3 Learn this drill to cross the road safely (4)
4 What Guides are doing! (7)
6 If you go orienteering you need to understand these (4)
7 All Queen's Guides must gain this Emblem (7)
10 Many Guides go on to .... Rangers (4)
12 A group of Ranger Guides form this (4)
13 Many Companies sing this at the end of the day (4)
14 Useful for catching things! (3)
17 Guides should try to keep this under control (6)
21 A roll to take to camp, but not to eat! (3)
23 Sailing Guides hope they won't be cast ...... (6)
24 Use this to clean up spills (3)
25 You could be a member of this flower of the field patrol (5)
26 Enjoyable way to take exercise (7)
28 It is more noble to do this, than to receive (4)
29 Initials of our Queen (1,1)
30 See 11 across
32 Part of the first Guide Law (5)
33 Christian name of the World Chief Guide (5)
35 If you don't do this, you will probably sink (4)

Solution on page 61

FACE THE MUSIC

a quiz by Ann Hillyer

Below are some famous composers' names which have got jumbled up. Can you untangle them and then pair them up with one of their famous musical compositions?

VIPEROOKF	**WATER MUSIC**
HENBEEVOT	**THE BLUE DANUBE**
HELAND	**TROUT QUINTET**
CHERUBST	**PETER AND THE WOLF**
SASSRUT	**MOONLIGHT SONATA**

Some garlic a day...

by Penny Morris

illustrated by Royston Edwards

We've all heard the saying 'an apple a day keeps the doctor away', but did you know that at one time people believed that eating garlic every day would keep them healthy? For thousands of years garlic has been used as medicine because it is such a fine natural antiseptic.

Garlic was used as long ago as 7,000 BC by the Babylonians, Ancient Egyptians, Hindus and Chinese. Ancient documents show that the Pharaohs spent the equivalent of £750,000 on garlic for the slaves who were building the great pyramids; the Bible also mentions that the pyramid builders were fed on garlic. In fact, the first known strike came about when the pyramid builders downed tools because their daily garlic ration failed to appear!

The Greeks, too, knew of the healing properties of garlic, and Aristotle, Hypocrates and Aristophanes all referred to it in their writings. Greek athletes pressed the juice from garlic and drank it by the glassful when training for the Olympic Games!

Galen (AD 131-200), a famous Roman physician, maintained that garlic was the finest antidote for any poison in the system. The Roman army, which incidentally was vegetarian, ate garlic in the belief that it would make them brave and courageous in battle. It seems more likely that the army doctors persuaded the men to eat garlic because they realised it would help keep them healthy. Soldiers used to rub a clove of garlic on to their wounds to reduce inflammation and promote healing.

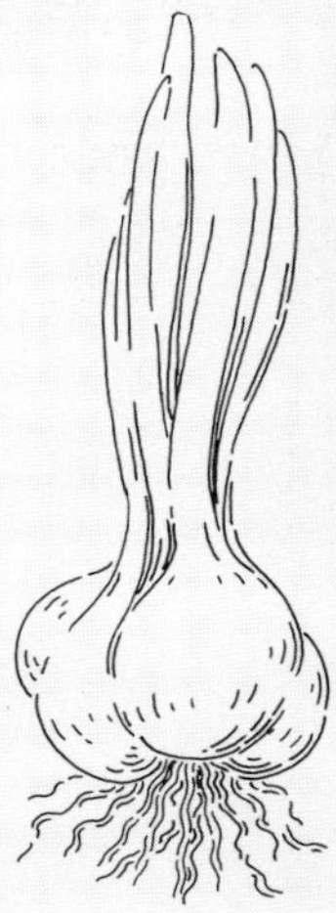

The French are famous for their use of garlic in the kitchen, but they also used it as a medicine in the past. In AD 1100 Robert of Normandy wrote, "Since garlic has the power to save from death, bear with it though it makes unsavoury breath."

In the eighteenth century it was discovered that drinking a potion of garlic and vinegar reduced the risk of catching the plague.

Victorian herbalists knew garlic as 'the prince of herbs' and used it as an antiseptic. Doctors would boil a mixture of garlic, vinegar and sugar and use the potion to treat asthma, colds, bronchitis, tuberculosis and whooping cough. The value of garlic passed into country lore, and on the farm, workers would keep a clove of garlic inside each sock to ward off colds.

Towards the end of the nineteenth century people stopped using garlic so much as it was replaced by new drugs, and for about fifty years it was hardly used as a medicine. But during the second world war Russian soldiers used it widely, and it was nicknamed 'Russian penicillin'. Garlic vapour is still used in many Russian hospitals.

More recently, medical research has found that both onions and garlic are remarkably effective in preventing blood clotting, and can be used to treat high blood pressure as well as helping people who suffer from catarrh and bronchitis.

It's a pity that garlic has rather an unfortunate reputation because of its strong smell; in fact the old saying could well be adapted to 'a garlic clove a day keeps everyone away'!

Recently an American woman tried to divorce her husband because she thought that he ate too much garlic! But if you chew a sprig of parsley after eating garlic you will find this removes the smell.

Garlic has always been popular in cooking and can transform a humble dish into a feast for the tastebuds. Next time you make cheese on toast try sprinkling chopped garlic over the cheese, then top it with sliced tomatoes and pop it under the grill for a few minutes. Delicious, and good for you, too!

HAND AND FOOT NOTES

by Shireen Bonner

illustrated by Jil Shipley

You probably take good care of your skin and hair and try to keep your figure trim, for the sake of good health and appearance. Yet how much time do you give to your hands, which are constantly on show, and to your feet, which are usually hidden away in shoes?

Feet are perhaps the most neglected part of your body, yet they have to support it! A complex structure of bones, muscles, sinews and nerves, feet can suffer permanent damage if continually mistreated, and any pain they feel can affect the rest of your body.

Your hands are often subjected to harsh treatment in the form of extreme temperatures and improper skin and nail care. To many people, hands reveal much of a person's character, so it is important to care for them, especially when going to interviews or meetings—bitten nails and dry skin do not make a very good first impression.

Adopt the following routines on a regular basis, and your hands and feet will thank you for it!

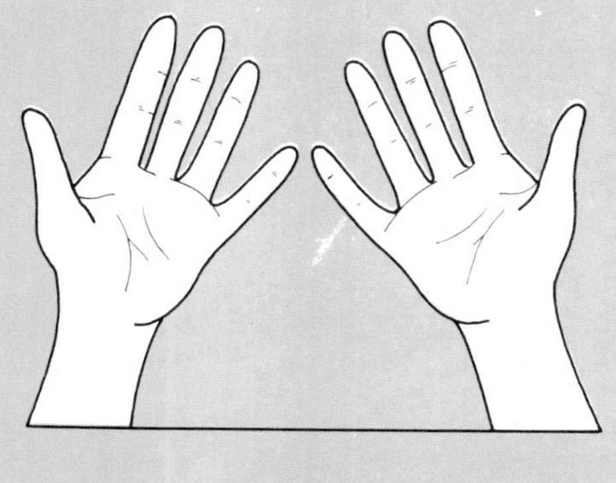

HANDS UP!

A common problem with hands is dry skin, which can result from exposure to cold or to dry heat, and from constant immersion in water. The moisture which is being stripped from your skin needs to be replaced. Always rinse the soap off your hands thoroughly after washing, and dry well, especially between the fingers, to prevent skin cracking. If you wear rings, make sure you dry under them. When washing dishes or doing a messy job such as cleaning brass, wear protective gloves. Hand lotion kept by the sink is a good reminder to moisturise your hands if they have been in soapy water for a while, and there are 'barrier' creams which protect your hands if you smooth the cream on ***before*** you tackle messy jobs. If your hands tend to be naturally dry, rub in a non-sticky hand lotion every night before bed, working the lotion over your wrists and elbows, too. Always wear gloves when it is cold outside—wind and cold cause red and dry hands, and can make them stiff.

Nails need constant care, as they are so exposed to damage, and brittle nails especially have a tendency to misbehave. Nails are composed of keratin, the same material as hair. Although the visible part of the nail is technically 'dead', the portion hidden by the cuticle is continually growing and regenerating. If you bite your nails, do make a concerted effort to stop. Easier said than done, but nail-biting is an off-putting and unhygienic habit, and however beautiful your hands are, ragged nails will ruin their appearance. Try using a suitably odious-tasting lotion to paint on your nails in an attempt to stop! Nails do not take too long to grow (about three to four weeks, often less) and it really is worth the wait. If your nails are brittle, eating a jelly cube a day may help.

Never bite the skin around your nails, or your cuticles, as this can cause painful and unsightly hangnails. Keep your nails trim—nails which are too long inevitably break—and file away any rough edges with an emery board. Clean under your nails ***carefully*** with an orange stick and gently ease the cuticles back when they are soft after washing. Any implement you use around your nails should be absolutely clean. If your nails seem unusually damaged and have white spots, are very ridged or discoloured, it would be advisable to consult your doctor.

Treat yourself to a manicure about once a week. Soak clean hands in a bowl of warm water with a few drops of baby shampoo and olive oil. Massage them gently in the water, then rinse well and dry thoroughly. Using nail clippers, trim the nails straight across and shape with an emery board, always filing in one direction at a time. Do not file while

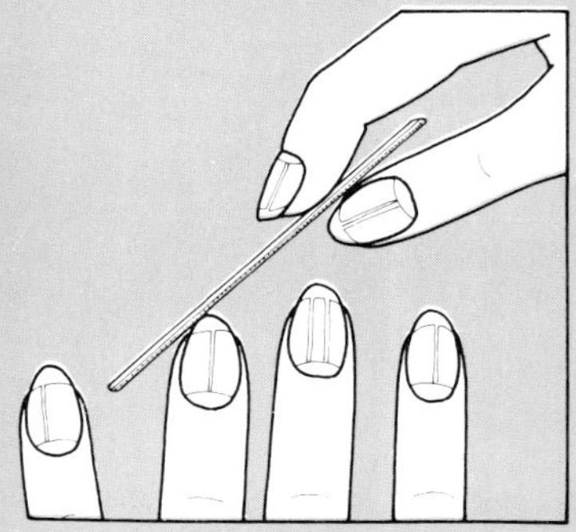

the nails are wet. Ease back the cuticles with an orange stick, being careful not to prod underneath them, then massage a liberal amount of cream into your hands. If you want to use nail varnish, ensure that your nails aren't greasy with cream, and paint on two coats of clear varnish. Alternatively, a nail buffer provides a healthy shine and stimulates the nail bed.

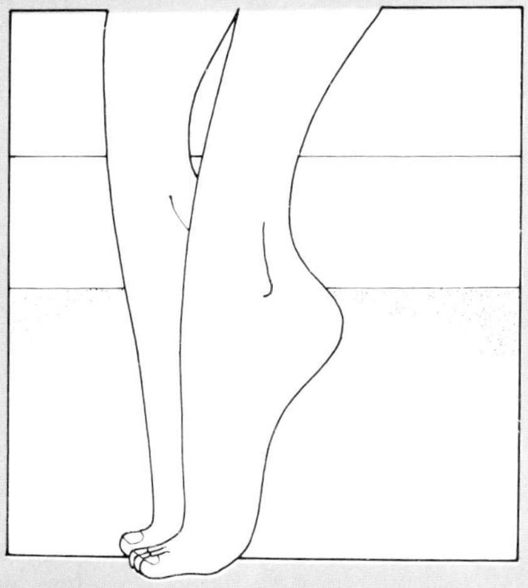

BEST FOOT FORWARD!

Feet enjoy a pedicure, but far more important is your treatment of your feet while they are actually hard at work, walking along unyielding pavements and cooped up in shoes and boots. Nine people in ten have foot problems, and these usually arise from ill-fitting shoes and improper care. You must look after your feet, especially when you are young, as some foot problems are not only painful and unattractive, but may need corrective surgery if allowed to persist. Women especially have been subjected to some tortuous footwear in the name of fashion, yet stiletto heels, pointed toes and synthetics aren't the only culprits—seemingly sensible shoes can cause corns and

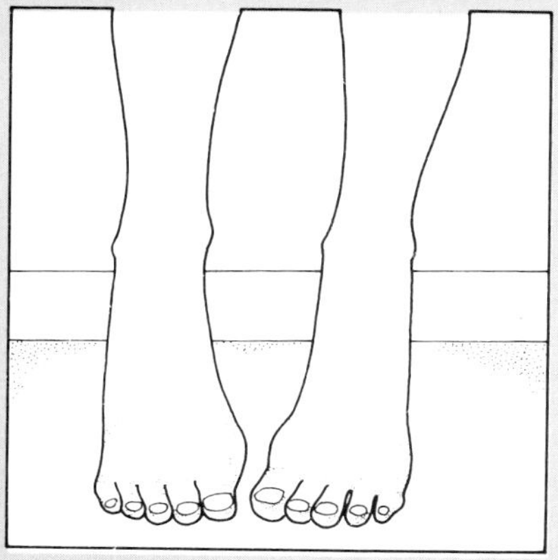

callouses too. Even ill-fitting tights and socks can cause friction and pressure which hardens the skin and may develop into a callous (normally found on the ball and heel of the foot). We ***have*** advanced in foot care a little; before the 1860s most shoes weren't made specifically for the left or right foot!

When you buy new shoes make sure they are comfortable—not just fashionable. Walk around in them, spring up and down to test their flexibility, and make sure you can spread your toes out comfortably. A well-fitting shoe should be half an inch longer than your foot and should fit snugly over the heel and instep. The uppers should be made of leather or a material which allows your feet to 'breathe'. Take care not to buy a pair which are too big as they may rub against your feet, causing blisters and corns. You will want to wear higher heels and backless shoes occasionally. If you do wear uncomfortable shoes for a while, pamper your feet when you get home by slipping into some sandals, or better still go barefoot where the ground is safe. Walking barefoot along a rough sandy beach not only feels good; the abrasive action of the sand helps smooth rough patches. Try not to wear the same pair of shoes two days running, to lessen the risk of foot odour.

Get used to a sensible foot care routine which begins with keeping your feet scrupulously clean, and always dry carefully, especially between the toes. Most toe nails need cutting at least once a month, and it is very important to cut them straight across, not too short, and don't round the corners, as this encourages in-growing toenails. File the nails and push back cuticles very carefully with an orange stick. If you do have any hard, dead skin on your feet, use a corn and callous file to gently remove it. A rough skin remover with a moisturiser works well, too. Pumice stones are useful for removing rough

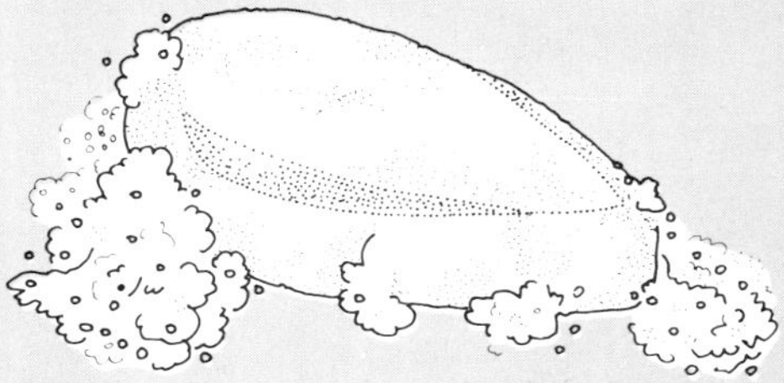

skin on feet, knees and elbows in the bath. Rub in some body lotion to keep your feet smooth, massaging it upwards from the toes towards the knees to aid circulation. Finally, a light dusting of talcum powder should keep your feet fresh all day, but if they are particuarly hot and tired you could use a foot spray. Remember that problems like athlete's foot and verrucae should be dealt with immediately—they are both highly

contagious. If you see any signs of a verruca (a foot wart that resembles a corn, and may have a black 'core') see your doctor. Athlete's foot can usually be controlled with products available from a chemist, but if in doubt, again consult your doctor. In either case, make sure the condition isn't spread to others by isolating towels and footwear and not walking barefoot. Never lend anyone your footwear while you have either condition. In fact, if you can avoid it, don't borrow or lend others' shoes at all. Make a regular check on your feet (especially between the toes and on the soles) particularly if you do a lot of sport. Changing rooms and swimming baths are ideal breeding grounds for lurking organisms!

Finally, feet and hands need exercise to keep them supple and shapely. Put aside a few minutes each day for these hand and foot exercises and you should feel the benefit quite quickly.

Standing or sitting, wriggle the toes of each foot separately for one minute. This helps to improve circulation and tone up muscles.

Imagine your toes are stuck to the floor. Grip with your toes and try to pull your foot away. Repeat two or three times with each foot. This helps both foot and leg muscles.

Sit in a comfortable chair and remove shoes. Keeping the rest of your leg as still as possible, slowly rotate each foot in turn. This helps to keep your ankles trim.

A similar exercise is good for your hands. Rotate each hand from the wrist, first clockwise, then anti-clockwise.

Playing the piano is a good way of exercising your hands. If you don't play, pretend! Stretch and wriggle your fingers to keep them supple. Remember, look after your hands and feet, because they look after ***you!***

LET'S GO BY CYCLE!

by Penny Morris

photographs by Frank Randall

Nowadays most people think of the bicycle as a fairly slow and safe method of transport, but when it was first invented, cycling was thought a most dangerous and unpleasant way to travel.

Cycling was popular with the first Guides. Here they are repairing a puncture.

The bicycle was first used as a means of transport at the end of the 18th century, but as long ago as 1493 Leonardo da Vinci had an idea for a similar machine. He drew a picture of a contraption with two wheels and handlebars, driven by pedals and a chain; it even had a system of gears. This drawing was discovered a few years ago in a library in Milan. Before it was found, historians believed the bicycle to have originated in France in the 18th century.

The ancestor of the modern bicycle was called a hobby horse, and was propelled by the rider using his feet on the ground. Hobby horses were quite popular in England, but they were more for fun than practical use. The first real bicycle was invented by a Scottish man called Kirkpatric Macmillan, in 1839. He rode quite long distances on it, but as it was made of wood and iron it was very heavy and clumsy. Then in the 1860s the Velocipede appeared. Nicknamed 'the Boneshaker', it was driven by cranks and pedals connected to the front wheel.

In 1869 three men cycled from London to Brighton, the first time such a journey had been made. The Times reported the event, saying that the 53 mile trip had taken 14 hours. Unfortunately it was possible to walk the same distance in only 11 hours, so it was not really good publicity for the bicycle! However, two months later another cyclist completed the journey in 7½ hours, restoring the reputation of the cycle!

The 'Penny Farthing' was introduced in 1871, with a large driving wheel and small rear wheel. Called the Ariel, it was the first really efficient cycle. Bicycling became a practical form of road transport as a cyclist could now outpace a horse-rider. Apart from horse power, the only other form of transport was the train, so bike riding was a very pleasant way to travel.

Riding a high cycle like the Ariel needed both skill and strong nerves. Getting on was difficult, while getting off safely was almost impossible! Going downhill was also dangerous as the bike had a tendency to pitch the rider forwards when brakes were applied, or if the front wheel hit a stone or rut.

As engineering techniques improved, the frames were made of hollow steel tubes, which made a great difference to the weight of the bike. Hollow wheel rims and ball bearings enabled bikes to run more smoothly, and as more people became interested Cycle Clubs were started up. Most clubs were based in cities and the members would cycle out into the countryside at weekends.

There were also tricycles around, which were much safer to ride and seemed likely to take over from bicycles until advances in design made them more reliable. The new 'safety bicycles' had wheels nearly equal in size, the rear wheel driven by a chain. Gears were introduced to make up for the smaller wheels. In 1888 a vet called John Boyd Dunlop patented his pneumatic tyre, the most important invention in the history of the bike. Compared with solid tyres, riding on pneumatic tyres was wonderful. They helped to increase the speed of the cycle as well as the comfort of the cyclist.

Originally, all bicycles had a crossbar, and so were not suitable for women to ride. Ankle length skirts made pedalling difficult, and tight corsets restricted the rider's breathing. Since women were determined to cycle, they started wearing loose-fitting woollen underwear, and silk knickerbockers. Skirts were raised by three inches, and made less full, but some women thought this was still too restricting and, following the example set by Amelia Bloomer, they took to wearing 'bloomers' instead of skirts. This was called 'rational' dress, and although the baggy bloomers reached well below the knee, many people thought they were indecent! Women wearing them were banned from hotel dining rooms and even had stones thrown at them. Eventually, however, rational dress was accepted, and the first women cyclists won a victory in the battle for the emancipation of women.

During the early part of this century cycling was the most popular form of transport. The bicycle was the fastest vehicle on the road, and was cheaper to keep than a horse. But after the arrival of the motor car the popularity of the cycle dwindled. For several decades the car has ruled the roads, but in recent years, with the escalation of fuel costs, increasing road congestion, and a growing concern over health matters, more and more people are realising that cycling provides an answer to these problems.

It's better by bike

The British Cycling Bureau are campaigning to persuade people that cycling is good for them and for their environment. A bicycle gives its rider independence. Once purchased it is cheap to run, and if cared for should last for years. Almost anyone, regardless of age and sex, can use a bike. It is quiet, does not create fumes, and poses little threat to other road users. Cycling is good exercise too, toning up the muscles and improving breathing.

There are several points to remember if you are a bicycle owner. Before setting out always check brakes, tyres and lamps, make sure the saddle and handlebars are the right height, and no nuts or bolts have worked loose. When you get your first bike, make sure it is the right size—don't get one that is too big. For safety, you should be able to put both feet on the ground while sitting astride the saddle. A bicycle with a crossbar is stronger than one without, so if you are a keen cyclist it is worth getting a boy's bike. Women racing cyclists always ride bikes with crossbars. Learn about cycle maintainance so that you can keep your bike in good condition.

Always remember to lock your bike when you leave it anywhere, if possible to a lamp-post or railing. Take any removable accessories with you. Keep a record of the frame number, and mark the bike with nail varnish or a hidden scratch so you can identify it quickly. You can get the frame stamped with your initials and postcode quite cheaply. Ask your local cycle dealer about having it done.

The only drawback to cycling is riding on busy roads, and car drivers are not always aware of cyclists. Dress conspicuously, and always give clear signals so motorists know what you intend to do. Check the Highway Code, so that you know the rules for cyclists, and if you can, get some training for riding in traffic, preferably by passing the National Cycling Proficiency Scheme. Whenever possible, try to find alternative routes, using quiet streets. If you don't own a bike, perhaps you could hire one. Write to the British Cycling Bureau, Stanhope House, Stanhope Place, London W2 2HH, for a list of hire companies.

Guiding in The Gambia

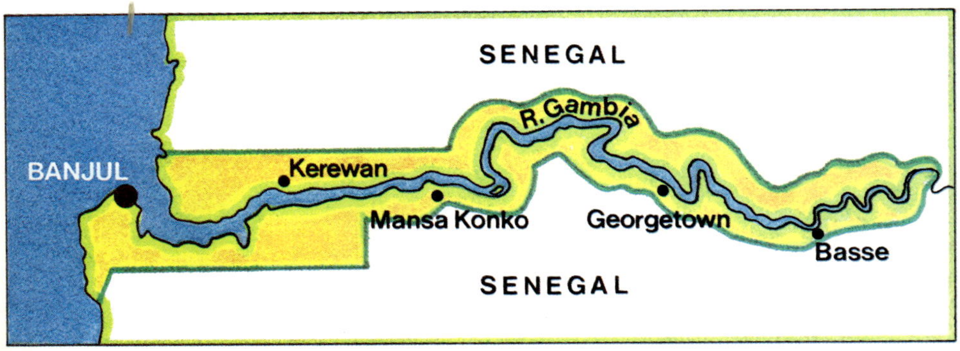

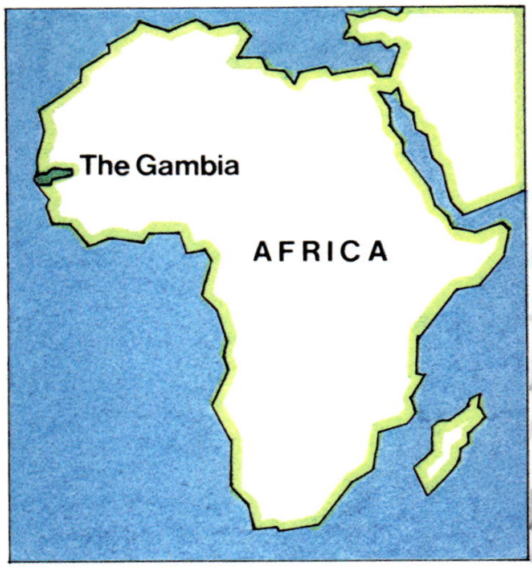

by Brenda Hughes

uniform by Kathleen Whapham
maps by Chris Sheridan

Photographs by Michael Redfern

One of the smallest countries in Africa, The Gambia is shaped like a long narrow slice of cake out of Senegal. It has a very short coast line from north to south, only 60km in length, but as this includes the mouth of the River Gambia it is in effect much longer. The Gambia consists of a strip of land each side of the river, being about 320km long and about 47km wide at the mouth of the river, narrowing to 24km further inland.*

Along the banks of the River Gambia are mangrove swamps and marshland, but further away from the river the country is wooded. The woodlands and river are the home of many animals. You might meet a herd of wild pigs or a family of monkeys or baboons, and see antelopes and jackals. Up river you might see hippopotamus and crocodile. The country is alive with birds, many of which you would recognise, like heron, doves, guinea fowl, hawks, warblers and duck, teal in particular. There is a Nature Reserve about 24km from the capital city, Banjul, where you could see many birds that would be new to you.

The wooded area is cleared in many places for crops. Rice is the main food crop, although ground nuts are the most important export. Rice is the staple food of the country and the people also eat fish, fruit and vegetables, and keep some domestic cattle. There is very little industry—the economy is primarily agricultural, but in recent years the tourist industry has been expanding.

The climate is tropical, with a rainy season from July to September, after which there is very high humidity lasting until late October. It is difficult to imagine what it is like: you feel damp all the time because although it is hot the heat is not dry, and when you perspire the moisture does not evaporate, but remains on your skin. If you wash, by the time you have dried yourself you feel wet again, and your skin remains hot and clammy. From November to

May the climate is hot and dry. Women have a life expectancy of 34 years and men 30; this contrasts with the Western average of 70 years.

The population contains a great mixture of ethnic groups including a few Europeans, Syrians and Lebanese, living mainly in and around Banjul. The main languages are Mandingo and Wolof, with English widely spoken as a second language. The majority of Gambians are Moslems, but in and around Banjul there are many Christians.

Guiding originally began in The Gambia in 1926, but only lasted a few years. The Movement was re-established in 1957 and has grown and progressed steadily since then. In 1966 The Gambia became an Associate Member of the World Association of Girl Guides and Girl Scouts, when the 19th World Conference, held in Japan, welcomed them as members.

The Gambian Guide and Brownie programmes are very much like ours. You would find it very easy to fit in with a Guide Company in The Gambia, although obviously the programme has been adapted to meet the needs and interests of the Gambian children. The Guides take a great interest in the community and play an active role in giving service wherever they can. They are always to the forefront on public occasions, giving help in a variety of ways. Service to the community consists of giving material assistance to the poor and sick. More and more young people are becoming interested in the Guide Movement in The Gambia.

You might like to find out more about The Gambia and feature it as a Patrol item on Thinking Day next year.

**Senegal and The Gambia united at the end of 1981 to form the new union of Senegambia.*

As nice as PIE!

by Doreen Fomi

illustrated by Ivan Ripley

If you are preparing to take your Cook's Badge, you may be thinking of making shortcrust pastry for part of clause 2. You can use pastry to make many different dishes. Why not try some of these?

First, make your pastry:

SHORTCRUST PASTRY

225g/8oz plain flour
½ level tsp salt
50g/2oz lard
50g/2oz block margarine or butter
5 dessertsps cold water

1 Sift the flour and salt into a mixing bowl.

2 Add the lard and margarine and cut into small pieces with a round-bladed knife. Rub the fats into the flour using your thumb and fingertips until the mixture looks like breadcrumbs. Do this very lightly so the mixture does not become yellow.

3 Add the water and stir with the round-bladed knife until the mixture begins to cling together. Then knead it lightly with one hand until it forms a ball.

4 The pastry is now ready to use. If you are not using it immediately put it into the fridge until it is needed.
In the following recipes, where it states 225g/8oz pastry, this means pastry made using 225g/8oz flour etc.

BACON, EGG AND CHEESE PIE

225g/8oz shortcrust pastry
4 rashers back bacon
3 eggs
1 slice white bread, crusts removed, grated into crumbs
100g/4oz grated Cheddar or Cheshire cheese
salt and pepper

1 Grease a 7'' sandwich tin with melted lard. Light the oven at Gas Regulo 6/200°C/400°F.

2 Cut the rind from the bacon, and cut into small pieces using kitchen scissors.

3 Put two of the eggs into a small pan with cold water and bring them to the boil, then turn the heat down and simmer for 10 minutes. Pour away the hot water, and run cold water over the eggs until they are cold.

4 Shell the eggs and chop them into pieces.

5 Mix the bacon, cheese and hard-boiled eggs in a basin.

6 Break the remaining egg into a cup and lightly beat with a fork. Add the beaten egg to the mixture in the basin, combining all the ingredients, and add the seasoning.

7 Roll out two-thirds of the pastry on a lightly floured board, keeping it in a circle as far as possible. When it is about 1½'' larger than the tin, fold it in half and carefully lift it into the tin. Open out and press firmly down round the inner edge and sides of the tin. Cut off the extra pastry and add it to the remaining third.

8 Put the cheese and egg mixture into the pie and spread it out.

9 Roll out the rest of the pastry until it is large enough to fit the top of the pie. Damp the edges of the pastry in the tin and then carefully lift the top onto the pie. Press the edges firmly together and cut away any extra pastry. Use any spare pastry to make leaves to decorate the top of the pie.

10 Place the pie on a baking tray and put it in the oven. Cook it at Gas Regulo 6/200°C/400°F for about 15 minutes until the top is pale brown, then lower the heat to Gas Regulo 4/180°C/375°F for a further 20 minutes (35-40 minutes in all).

11 Serve hot or cold with a green vegetable and mashed potato, or salad.

CORNED BEEF AND VEGETABLE PIE

This pie is similar to the one above but with a different filling. It is a good way to use up left-over vegetables.

225g/8oz shortcrust pastry
350g/12oz tin of corned beef, cubed
225g/8oz of left-over cooked vegetables (potato, carrot, beans, peas, cabbage, etc.)

1 Light the oven at Gas Regulo 6/200°C/400°F.

2 Line a 7'' sandwich tin as for the Bacon, Egg and Cheese Pie.

3 In a mixing bowl, combine the corned beef and vegetables with a fork, seasoning with salt and pepper.

4 Put the mixture in the pie and cover with the remainder of the pastry as above.

5 Cook as the Bacon, Egg and Cheese Pie.

YORKSHIRE APPLE PIE

225g/8oz shortcrust pastry
400g/1lb cooking apples, peeled, cored and sliced
50g/2oz sugar

100g/4oz Cheddar cheese, thinly sliced

1 Divide the pastry in half and with one half line an 8 or 9" pie plate.

2 Put the slices of apple onto the pastry with the sugar, and then cover with the slices of cheese.

3 Roll out the remaining pastry and cover the pie.

4 Cook as the Bacon, Egg and Cheese Pie.

Not all pies are made using pastry. You can cover savoury pies with potato:

SAUSAGE PIE

400g/1lb skinless pork sausages
400g/1lb potatoes
1 level tsp salt
300g/12oz tin tomatoes
25g/1oz lard
2 medium onions
25g/1oz margarine or butter
a little milk
salt and pepper

1 Light the oven at Gas Regulo 4/180°C/375°F.

2 Peel the potatoes, cut them into quarters and put them in a saucepan with a teaspoon of salt and enough cold water to cover. Bring to the boil, then simmer for 20 minutes.

3 While the potatoes are cooking, skin the onions and chop them finely. Melt the lard in a frying pan and gently fry the onion until soft, then remove it from the pan with a draining spool, and put it in an oven-proof dish.

4 Test the potatoes with a knife; when they feel soft they are ready. Drain and mash them with the margarine or butter, milk and salt and pepper.

5 Fry the sausages in the pan the onions were fried in, or if you prefer, grill them. When cooked, cut them into one-inch pieces and put them in the dish with the onions.

6 Pour the tin of tomatoes over the sausages, breaking them up to spread them evenly.

7 Cover the pie with the mashed potato, neatening it with a fork.

8 Put the pie on a baking tray in the oven for about half an hour to heat through and lightly brown the potato. This pie can be made in advance and kept in the fridge for a day, in which case it may need slightly longer to heat through.

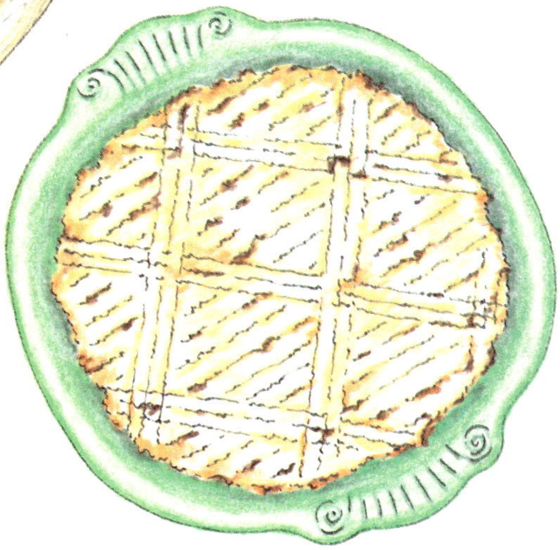

TUNA BAKE

This is a very quick and easy pie—very satisfying on a cold day!

1 large tin tuna
1 large tin condensed mushroom soup
400g/1lb cooked potatoes, mashed with a little milk and margarine or butter

1 Light the oven at Gas Regulo 4/180°C/375°F.

2 Open the tin of tuna and drain off the oil. Put the tuna in a basin and break it up with a fork.

3 Open the soup and pour it over the tuna, mixing the two with a fork.

4 Season with salt and pepper, then put the mixture into an oven-proof pie dish.

5 Carefully put the mashed potato on top and smooth it with a fork.

6 Put the pie on a baking tray and put it in the oven for 30-40 minutes, until it is heated through and lightly browned on top.

7 Serve with a green salad or carrots.

APPLE BUNS

225g/8oz plain flour
1 tsp cream of tartar
½ tsp bicarbonate of soda
pinch of salt
100g/4oz block margarine
100g/4oz sugar
1 egg
1 cup of stewed apple
caster sugar

1 Light the oven at Gas Regulo 6/200°C/400°F.

2 Sift the flour, tartar and soda into a mixing bowl.

3 Add the margarine to the flour and cut it into small pieces with a round-bladed knife, then rub the fat into the flour until it resembles fine breadcrumbs.

4 Stir in the sugar, then add the egg and mix to a soft dough, using one hand.

5 Flour your work surface and rolling pin and turn out the dough.

6 Cut the dough in half, and roll out one half until it is about ¼" thick.

7 With a round pastry cutter, cut out rounds of the dough and put them into a lightly-greased bun tin.

8 Put a spoonful of apple into each bun.

9 Roll out the rest of the dough, adding any trimmings from the first rolling, and with a smaller cutter, cut out tops for the buns. Put a lid on each and press the edges together.

10 Put the bun tin in the oven for 10-15 minutes until the buns are lightly browned. Remove the tin from the oven and sprinkle the buns with caster sugar. When they have cooled slightly take them out of the tin and put them on a wire tray to cool further.

These amounts make approximately 24 buns, so if you have a bun tin which will hold 12, put the rest of the dough mixture in the fridge until you have made the first batch.

Fashion Makes

by Jil Shipley

All these clothes will fit sizes 10-14. They are meant to be generously cut —the trousers and skirt can be made larger or smaller simply by altering the side seams. The jacket needs to be roomy, and the top is pulled in at the waist so that it will fit all sizes.

Make the patterns from wrapping paper or special dressmaker's drafting paper, which is ready marked

with a grid and will make the job much easier; buy it in sheets from sewing departments of large stores. Remember that each square on this grid represents 2cm. Copy the pattern carefully, using a set square. All pieces have a 1cm seam allowance, unless marked otherwise. Pockets can be used or not, as you please. Position the pockets anywhere you like.

Experiment with colours and fabrics—make the whole outfit in one fabric but three colours, use two similar prints, or the same print in two or three colours. Or make the jacket in one fabric with the facing and cuffs in a different colour. If you want to do this, when you are making the jacket pattern, cut from a to b and add 1cm to each edge so that you have a separate cuff pattern.

All raw edges must be neatened, and remember to press each seam as you go along. Tack whenever you are unsure.

The fabric amounts required are given for 90cm fabric.

Making up

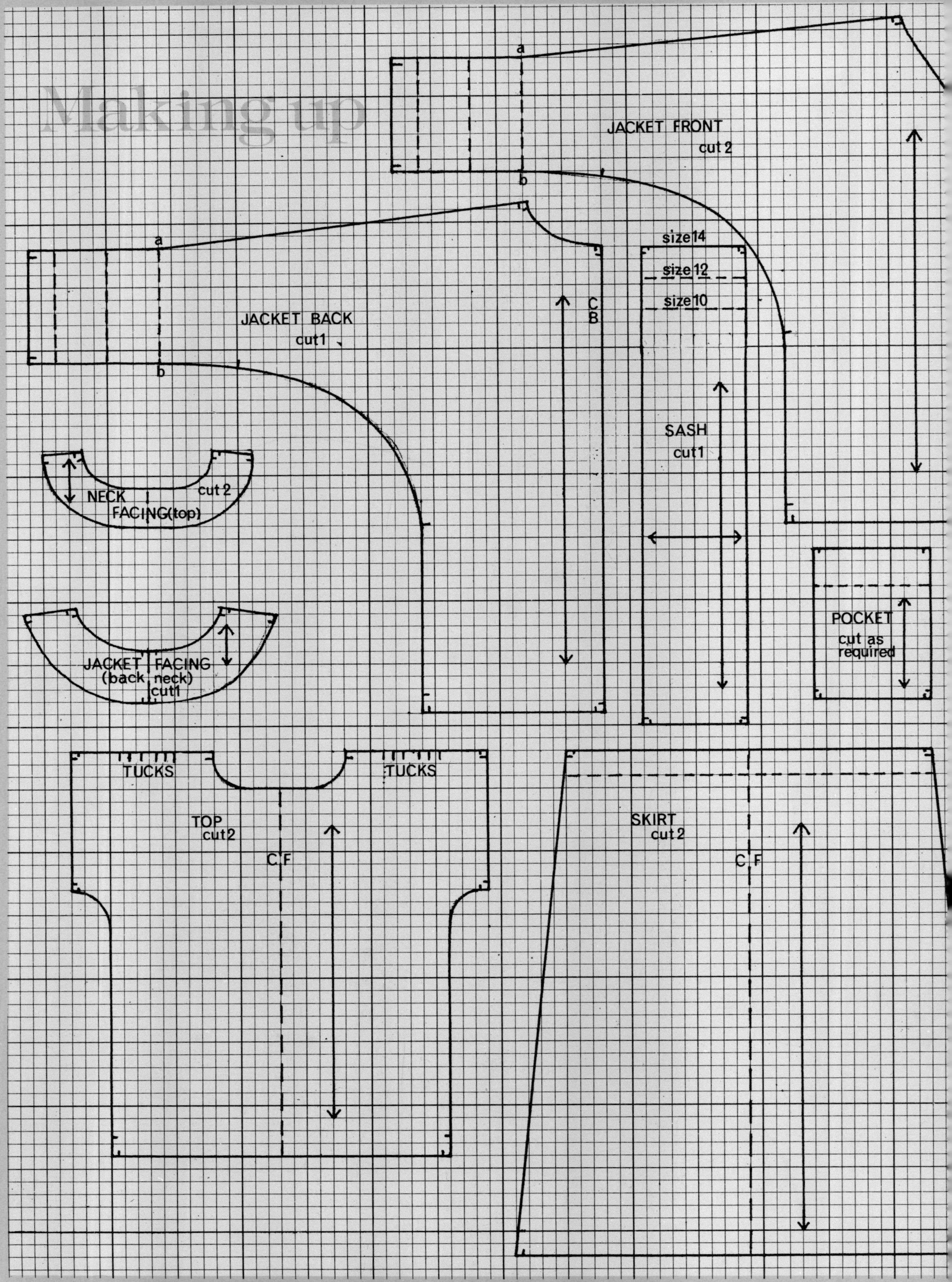

a
JACKET FRONT
cut 2
b
a
JACKET BACK
cut1
b
C
B
size14
size 12
size10
SASH
cut1
NECK
FACING(top)
cut 2
POCKET
cut as
required
JACKET FACING
(back neck)
cut1
TUCKS
TUCKS
TOP
cut2
C F
SKIRT
cut 2
C F

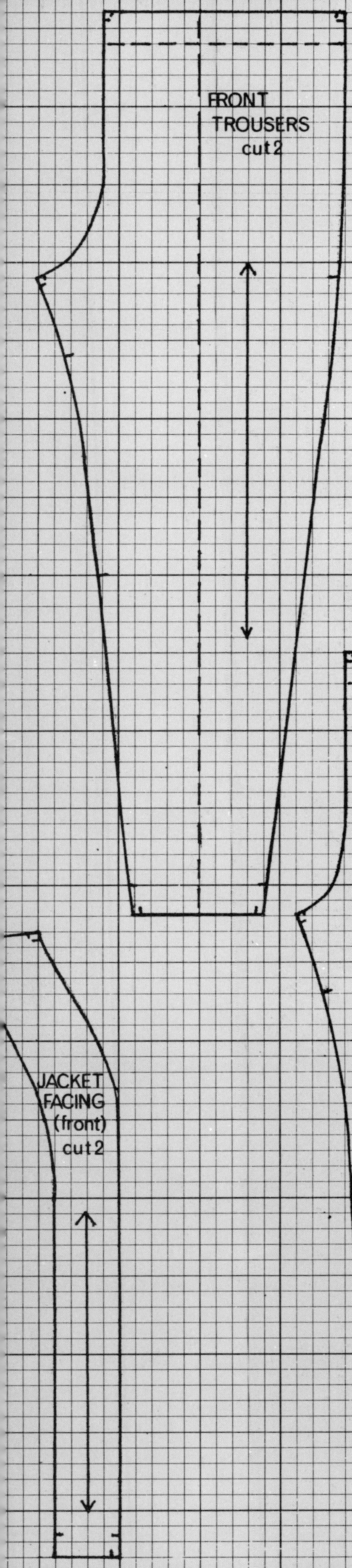

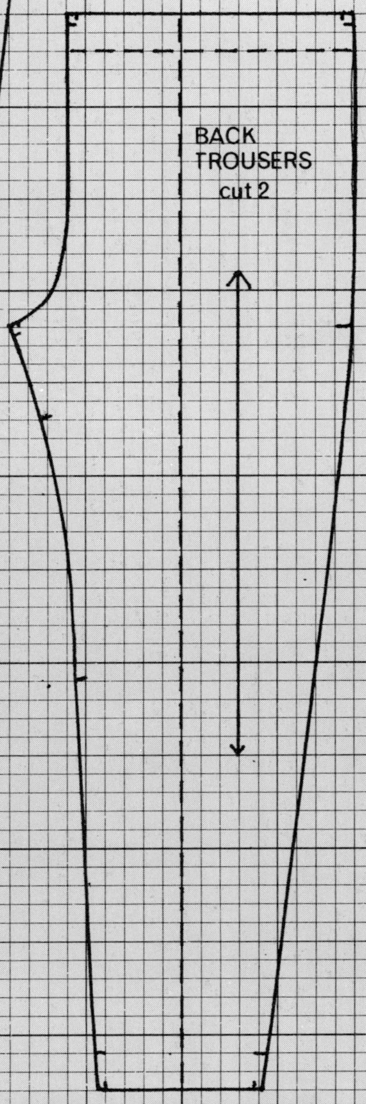

The jacket: Using one-way fabric the jacket takes 4.10m; using two-way fabric 3.30m. If you are using contrasting fabric for the cuffs and facings it takes 3.20m (one-way fabric) or 2.20m (two-way fabric) and 90cm for the contrast facings.

Cut out two backs, two fronts, two back facings and two front facings, and pockets if required. Join the jacket pieces at CB (centre-back), side seams and shoulder seams. Press and neaten the raw edges. Join the facing pieces at CB and shoulder seams. Press and neaten. Place right-side facing to right-side jacket and sew. Trim the turning, snip where necessary and press. Join facing to the shoulder seam with two or three herringbone stitches or catch-stitch. Hem cuffs, fold on fold lines and press back. Catch stitch at underarm seam. Hem the jacket. Press and try it on—decide where you want the pockets and sew them on.

The pockets: Turn down 6cm at the top edge of the pocket and 1cm around the other three edges. Press. Pin into position as required and sew onto the garment.

The top: The top takes 1.40m of fabric. Cut two pieces—the back and front are exactly the same. Sew two tucks in each shoulder where marked (or gather the shoulder line between tuck marks) to reduce the shoulder line to 14cm. Cut two facings. Sew up top shoulder seams and facing shoulder seams, and neaten. Place right-side facing to right-side garment and stitch together. Trim the turnings, snip where necessary and turn through. Neaten the raw edges and secure to the shoulder seams with herringbone or catch-stitch. Hem the armhole and the bottom edge of your top. Press.

The skirt: The skirt takes 1.6m of fabric—less if you're making it shorter (two times your finished skirt length plus 8cm). Cut two pieces; the back and front are exactly the same. Sew up the side seams, press and neaten. Press down 1cm at the waist edge, then 3cm, and stitch a 3cm casing for the elastic. Cut the elastic to fit your waist plus a 4cm overlap, and insert it into the casing. Position and sew on the pockets, if required.

The trousers: The trousers take 2.40m of fabric (less if you are short: two times the waist to hem measurement plus 16cm). Cut out two back and front pieces. Sew the back crutch seam together, sew the front crutch seam together, snip the seams and neaten. Press. Join the side seams, press and neaten. Join the inside leg seam, press and neaten. Press down 1cm at the waist edge, then 3cm and stitch a 3cm casing for the elastic. Cut the elastic to fit your waist plus a 4cm overlap and insert it into the casing. Hem the trousers and press.

The sash: Cut a piece of fabric the size of your waist plus a 6cm overlap. It should be 16cm wide. Hem all the edges. Make four tucks at each end of the sash to reduce the width to 5cm. Stitch down the tucks for 2cm, so that you have a firm piece of fabric at either end of the sash measuring 5cm by 3cm. Stitch Velcro onto the sash ends for fastening.

gadgets

by Helen Ryan and Ann Walker

FURNISH YOUR SLEEPING TENT

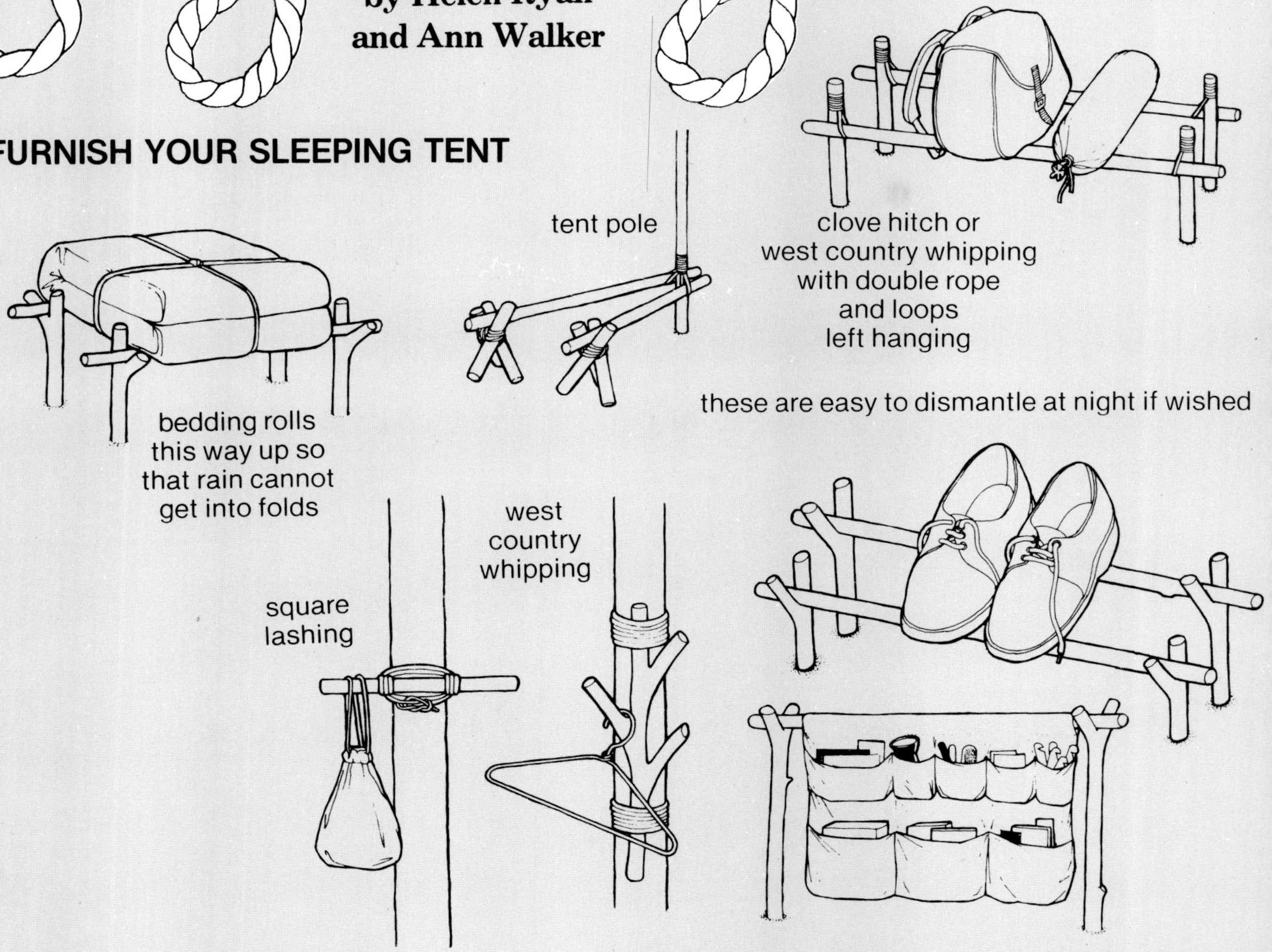

FURNISHING THE WASH AREA

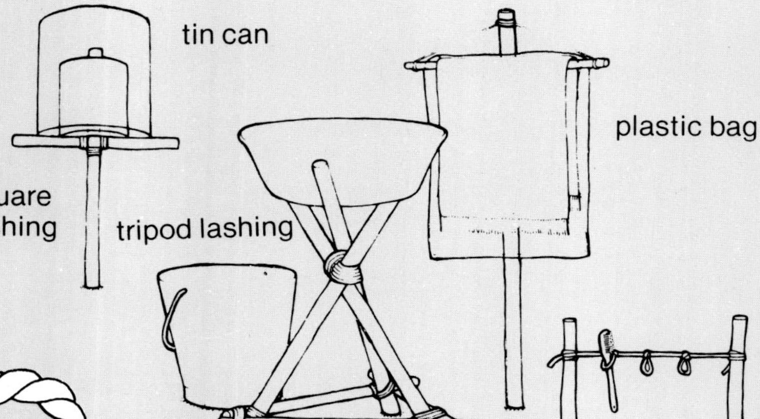

HINTS FOR GADGET-MAKING

*Use green wood: cherry, hazel, ash and birch are among the best woods to use.
*Forks should be shaped like

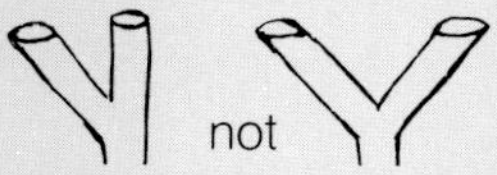

*Square lashing or loops as shown above can be used if forked sticks are not available.
*Saw off any sharp ends of wood which may damage people or equipment.
*Some gadgets (eg small tripods) can be made before going to camp. Point the end of any wood which goes into the ground; make a hole with a tent peg so that it will go in more easily. Position gadgets so that they never rub against canvas. Dismantle gadgets carefully to preserve both string and wood for the next camp.

A gadget is a device which makes life in camp easier, tidier or more comfortable. Instructions for all knots and lashings shown are given in *Help Yourself to Knotting* (GGA publication).

FURNISHING THE KITCHEN AREA

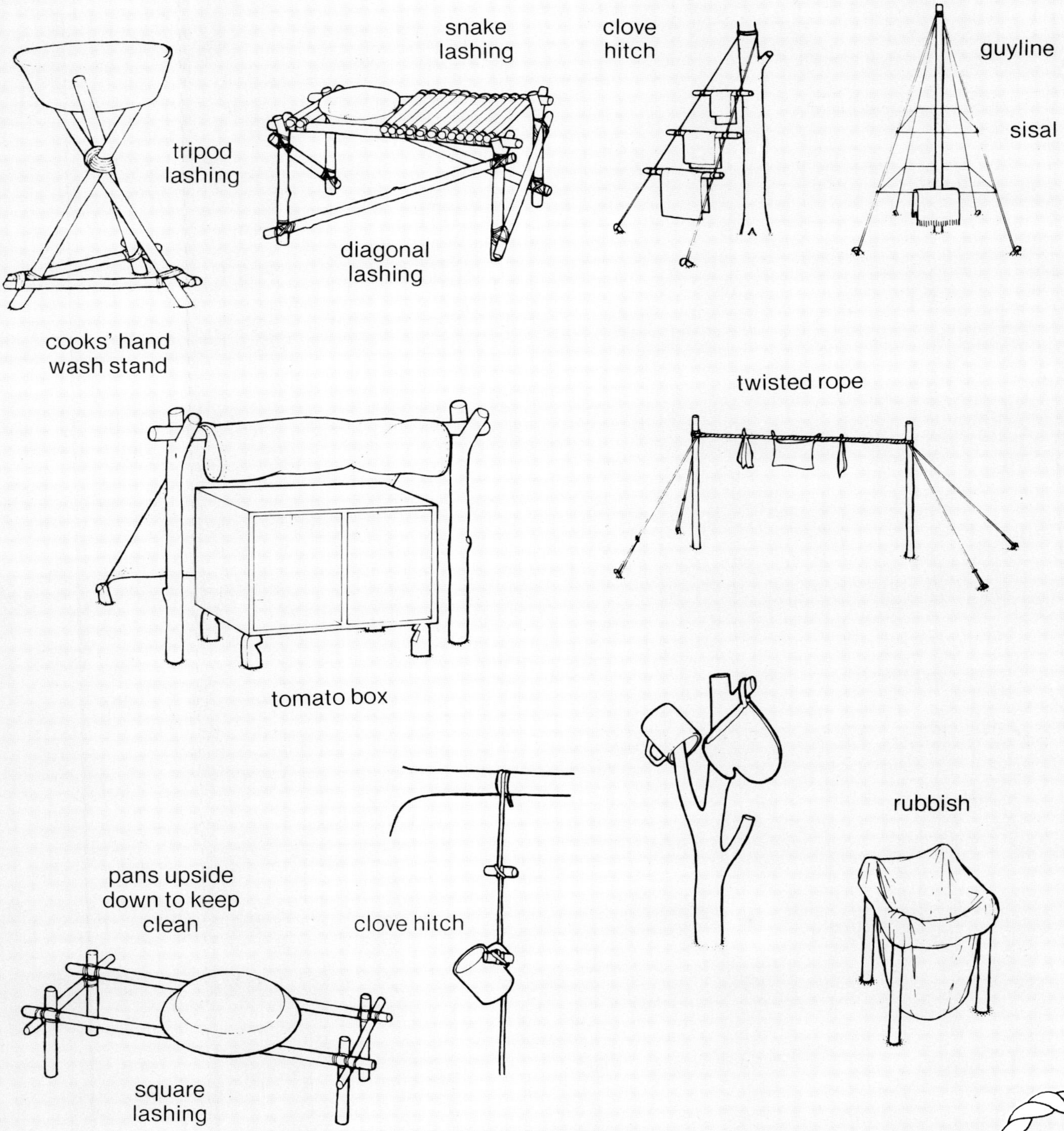

illustrated by Chris Sheridan

STARGAZING

by Dorothy Slyfield

illustrated by Chris Sheridan

When you look up at the sky on a clear, dark night, do you ever wonder just what you are gazing at? Perhaps you intend to find a book on astronomy the next day? That, and a pencil and notebook, are all you need to start with—additional equipment can be acquired later.

Here are some hints to help you start

*Take a groundsheet, rug and torch, and lie down outside. If you are indoors, make sure you can't fall out of the window!
*Avoid strong artificial light or you won't see much in the sky.
*Start fairly soon after dark, when only the brightest stars are visible—too many stars can be confusing.
*Concentrate on identifying two or three constellations in one part of the sky, then try to identify others in the same area.
*If you have borrowed a telescope or binoculars keep them steady, preferably on a tripod. NEVER use either to look at the SUN as even a one-second glance could seriously damage your eyes!
*Take a pencil, not a ballpen. A pencil will write at any angle, even on damp paper.
*When recording your observations, squared paper will help you plot positions accurately. Record your observations weekly and note the date, time, compass direction, latitude and weather conditions. Anything unusual can be checked later. From your records, it will seem that the stars move, but it is really our planet Earth which rotates, taking 23 hours 56 minutes to complete an orbit. This is why we see the same constellation four minutes earlier each day, about half-an-hour earlier each week and two hours earlier each month!

Constellations are groups of stars which appear to travel together although actually they may be separated by millions of light years. Reliable star maps show their positions at all times of the year. In the UK we see northern circumpolar constellations all the time, middle heaven constellations part of the time, but we never see southern circumpolar constellations.

*Photographs of constellations taken using a tripod-mounted camera with locked-open shutter and fast film show 'star trails', short bands of light indicating the path each star has travelled whilst the shutter was open.
*Photographs or slides will help with identification. Get someone to help you take photographs to show your Patrol.
*Use thick and thin needles to prick the pattern of a constellation through a blank black colour slide, or black paper, then look through it.

The Ancient Greeks named the constellations and wrote myths and legends about them. They classified stars by their magnitude, or brightness. A first magnitude star is two-and-a-half times as bright as a second magnitude star, which is two-and-a-half times as bright as a third, and so on.

Stars seem to be different colours. The colour depends on the star's temperature, which depends on its chemical composition, and colours range from blue-white, white, yellowish-white and yellow to orange and red.

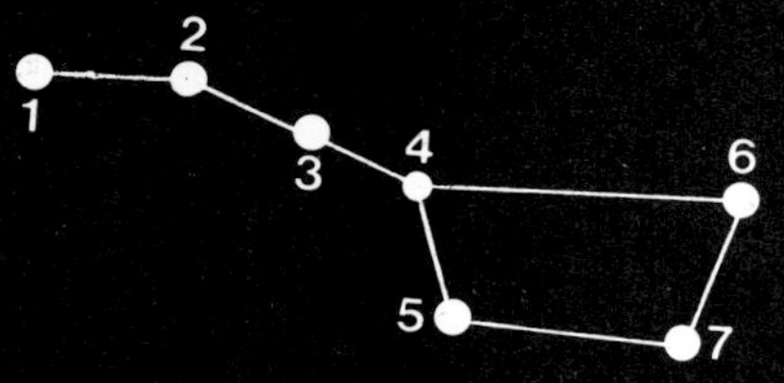

URSA MAJOR
(Great Bear, Plough, Charles' Wain)

This constellation, one of the very oldest, was known by several names, one of which was Callisto. In Greek myth Callisto was an attendant to the goddess Juno, daughter of King Lycaon. Callisto was so beautiful that she surpassed even Juno, who became enraged with jealousy. To protect Callisto, Jupiter turned her into a bear, but her son Arcas saw the bear when he was hunting, and was just about to kill it when Jupiter intervened and turned Arcas into a bear as well (Ursa Minor) and then placed both animals in the sky.

Of the seven principal stars in Ursa Major, six are of second magnitude. Mizar is a 'double star'—a smaller star called Alcor can be seen very close to it. Merak and Dubhe are known as the pointers as they always point to Polaris, the (north) Pole Star, an accurate guide for navigators to steer by.

Star name	Magnitude	Colour
1* Alkaid	2	blue-white
2* Mizar	2	white
3* Alioth	2	white
4* Megrez	3	white
5* Phad	2	white
6* Dubhe	2	yellow
7* Merak	2	white

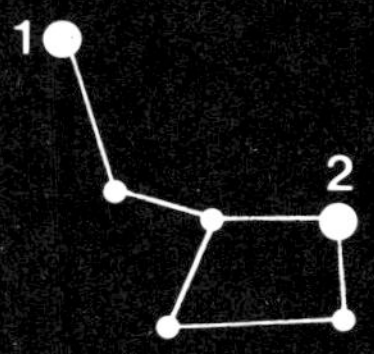

URSA MINOR (Little Bear)

The seven main stars in Ursa Minor form a smaller replica of Ursa Major. The most important, Polaris, is the closest to the north celestial pole. Kocab is interesting for its orange colour.

Star name	Magnitude	Colour
1* Polaris	2	yellowish-white
2* Kocab	2	orange

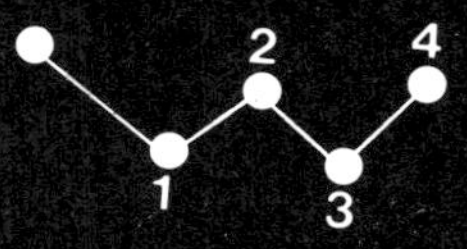

CASSIOPEA (The Queen)

In legend, this constellation represents Queen Cassiopea, wife of King Cepheus and mother of Princess Andromeda. Cassiopea angered Neptune, the sea-god, by saying that Andromeda was more beautiful than Neptune's sea nymphs, the Nereids. Neptune sent a monster to destroy Cepheus' land and the despairing king and queen consulted the oracle. The oracle pronounced that Andromeda be chained to a rock and left as food for the monster, but in the nick of time she was saved by the gallant hero Perseus.

Cassiopea is recognised by the W formed by its five main stars, several of which are 'variable', ie their magnitude is not constant.

Star name	Magnitude	Colour
1* Ruchbah	2-3	white
2* Gamma	2	blue-white
3* Shedir	2-3	reddish
4* Caph	2-3	yellowish-white
5* Segin	5-6	white

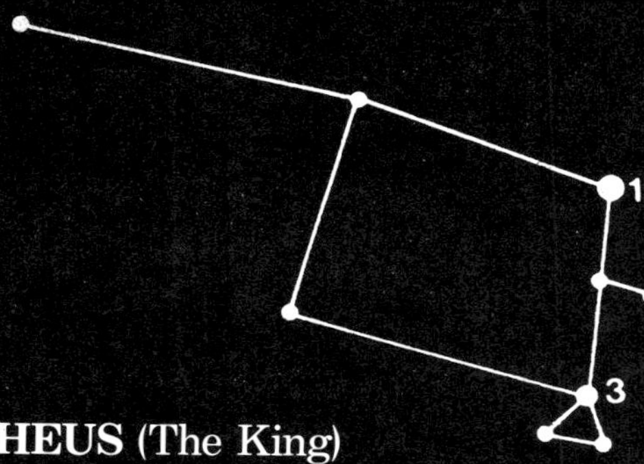

CEPHEUS (The King)

This constellation is difficult to find. It forms a triangle with two smaller stars which are of variable magnitude over a period of five to six days. You will need binoculars to see the Garnet star which is a spectacular red.

Star name	Magnitude	Colour
1* Alderamin	2	white
2* Garnet	4-6	red
3* Cephei	3-4	white

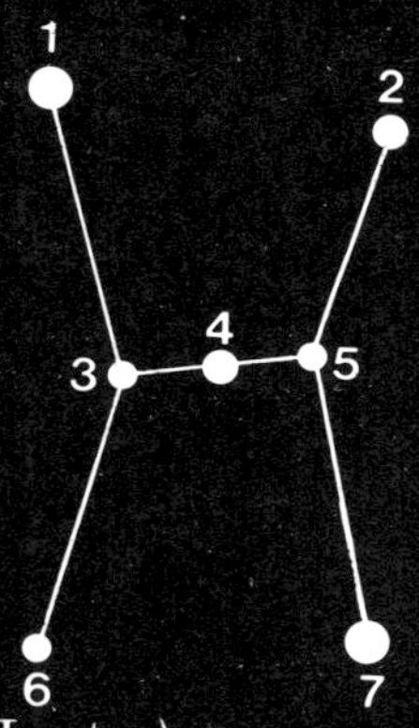

ORION (The Hunter)

In legend, Orion was in love with the goddess Diana, much to the annoyance of Apollo. Apollo persuaded Diana to try her skill, by shooting at a distant mark in the sea, which proved to be Orion's head! Having killed him with her arrow, Diana placed him among the stars.

Star name	Magnitude	Colour
1* Betelgeuse	1	red
2* Bellatrix	2	white
3* Alnitak	3	white
4* Alnilam	2	white
5* Mintaka	3	white
6* Saiph	3	white
7* Rigel	1	blue-white

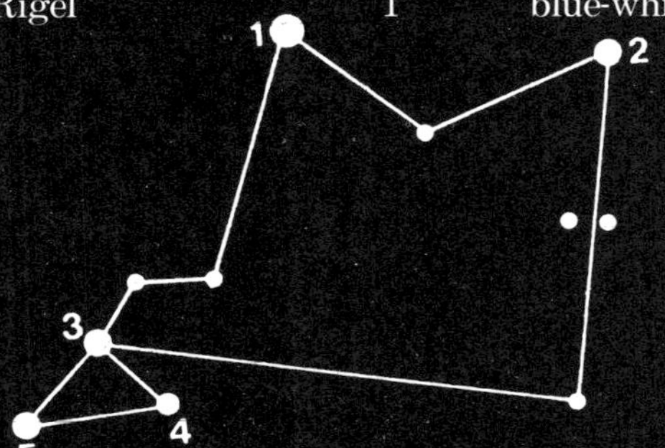

CANIS MAJOR (Great Dog)

This constellation represents one of Orion the

Hunter's dogs (the other being Canis Minor), faithful companions to their master during his never-ending journeys across the sky.

Canis Major has within it Sirius (The Dog Star), the brightest star, and is best seen during winter.

Star name	Magnitude	Colour
1* Sirius	1	white
2* Mirzam	2	blue-white
3* Wezea	2	yellowish-white
4* Adara	3	blue-white
5* Aludra	2	blue-white

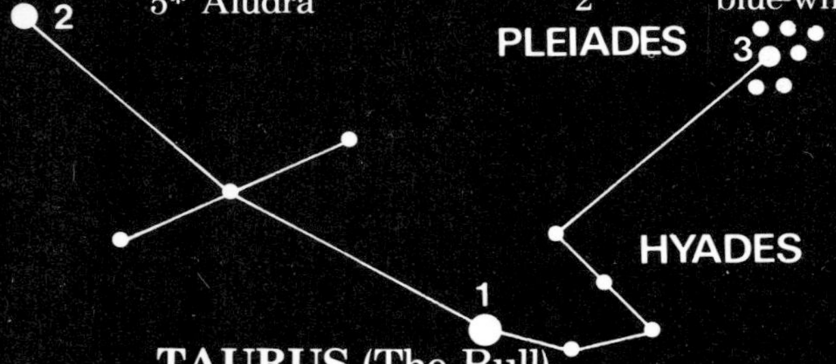

TAURUS (The Bull)

This is one of the constellations of the Zodiac. Jupiter fell in love with Europa, daughter of the King of Crete. He turned himself into a white bull, persuaded Europa to ride on his back, and dashed into the sea and swam off with her!

Taurus contains two spectacular star clusters, the Pleiades and the Hyades. The Pleiades are also known as the Seven Sisters but on a cold, clear night you may see more than seven. The Hyades are more widely scattered around Aldebaran, a large red star known as 'the red eye of the bull'.

Star name	Magnitude	Colour
1* Aldebaran	1	red
2* Alnath	2	blue-white
3* Alcyone	3	blue-white

The nine planets require careful observation as they circle around the sun, each one following its own well-known course. Unlike the twinkling stars, planets shine with a steady light, which is in fact a reflection of the Sun's rays. Here is a table you may find interesting.

Planet	Distance from Sun in kilometres	Time taken to go round Sun	Diameter in kilometres	Number of known moons
MERCURY	57,600,000	88 days	4,800	0
VENUS	107,200,000	224¾ days	12,320	0
EARTH	148,800,000	365¼ days	12,682	1
MARS	226,400,000	687 days	6,720	2
JUPITER	772,800,000	11¾ years	141,920	13
SATURN	1,417,600,000	29 years	120,160	9
URANUS	2,852,800,000	84 years	46,880	5
NEPTUNE	4,468,800,000	164¾ years	50,400	2
PLUTO	5,865,600,000	248 years	5,900	0

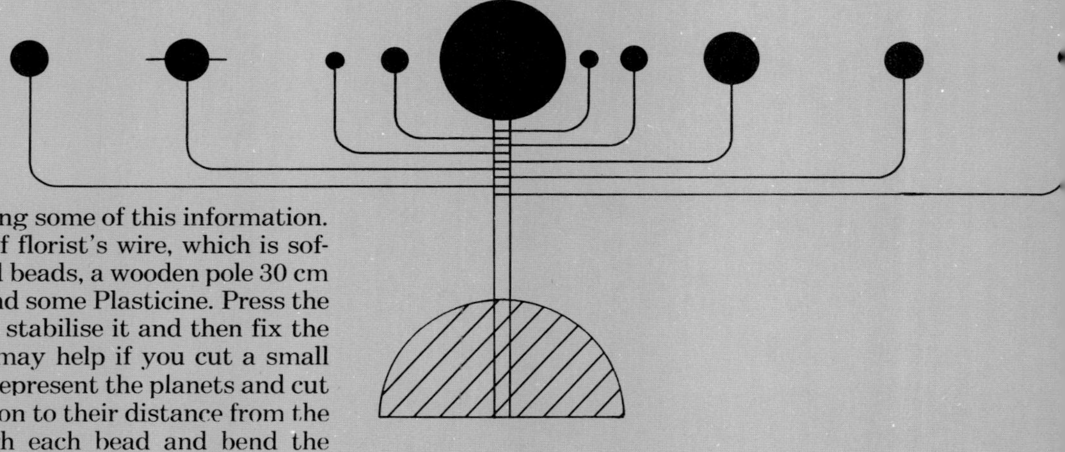

You can make a model using some of this information. I suggest you use a reel of florist's wire, which is softish, various sizes of round beads, a wooden pole 30 cm long, a table tennis ball, and some Plasticine. Press the pole into the Plasticine to stabilise it and then fix the ball (the Sun) on top—it may help if you cut a small hole in it. Select beads to represent the planets and cut lengths of wire in proportion to their distance from the Sun. Thread wire through each bead and bend the sharp end back over the bead to hold it securely. Twist the other end of the wire round the pole as close to the ball as possible.

The Solar System also includes three groups of lesser bodies: asteroids (minor planets) which you cannot hope to see with the naked eye; comets, which look like stars with a long tail; and meteors or 'shooting stars'. If you happen to be in the south of England, or better still the Canary Islands, between January and April in 1986 you may catch a glimpse of Halley's Comet which reappears every 76 years.

If you become really interested in this subject, you may like to join the Society for Junior Astronomers. Write to the Secretary, the British Astronomical Association, 58 Vaughn Gardens, Ilford, Essex IG1 3PD, for information and an enrolment form. You would also find a visit to the National Maritime Museum at Greenwich extremely helpful. Make sure you visit the Observatory there.

Useful references

The Night Sky Daily Telegraph Map Series
The Observer's Book of Astronomy Patrick Moore
The Ladybird Book of the Night Sky Mary T. Brück
Signpost to the Stars F.E. Butler
The Night Sky—articles published on the first of each month in The Times

Have you got your Star Gazer Badge yet?

To find out the syllabus, write to the Programme and Training Secretary at Girl Guide Headquarters, 17-19 Buckingham Palace Road, London SW1W 0PT.

COOKERY DO!

devised by Cecilia Fellner

illustrated by Chris Sheridan

1. Which are better for you and taste best, white or brown-shelled eggs?

2. Eggs are best when newly-laid —true or false?

3. Your fish fingers have turned out soggy and greasy. What went wrong?
   a) fat not hot enough?
   b) too many in the pan at once?
   c) insufficiently drained?

4. What can you use to remove a mark made by a ballpen?

5. To ensure glacé icing will shine when dry, do you:
   a) smooth it with a hot knife?
   b) cool the cake in the fridge?
   c) stir in a small knob of butter?

6. Which will you need flour to make?
   a) an omelette?
   b) a pancake?
   c) meringues?
   d) a soufflé?

7. How can you avoid meringues sticking to the baking tin? Should you
   a) brush the tin with cooking oil?
   b) line the tin with greaseproof paper?

8. Which is the cockle, mussel, whelk, prawn, oyster?

9. The liver you have cooked tastes bitter. Before cooking, should you have
   a) sprinkled it with sugar?
   b) sprinkled it with lemon juice?
   c) used less salt?

10. Painting a room, in which order should you paint:
   a) woodwork
   b) ceiling
   c) walls

11. Who wrote: 'C-l-e-a-n, clean, verb active, to make bright, to scour. W-i- n, win, d-e-r, der, winder, a casement.'? When the boy knows this he goes and does it.

12. What is French dressing for and what does it consist of?

13. Should you store eggs with the pointed ends up or down?

14. Who wrote: 'Tis an ill cook that cannot lick his own fingers.'?

15. How would you describe:
   a) a hamburger
   b) a frankfurter
   c) a Wiener Schnitzel
   d) a ragoût
   e) a bouquet garni
   f) a marinade

16. Who wrote: 'Kissing don't last— cookery do!'

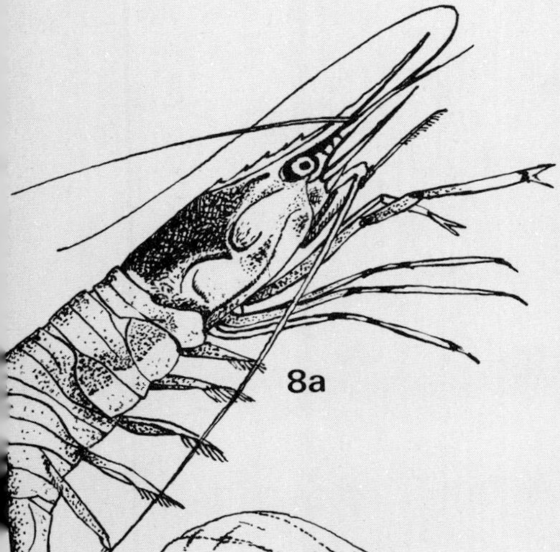
8a

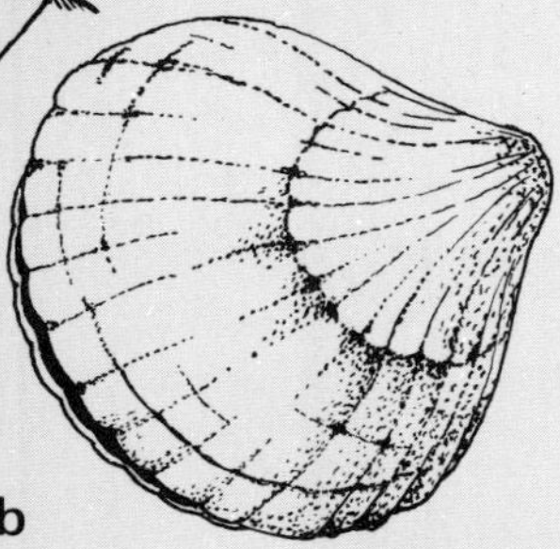
8b

8e

11

6

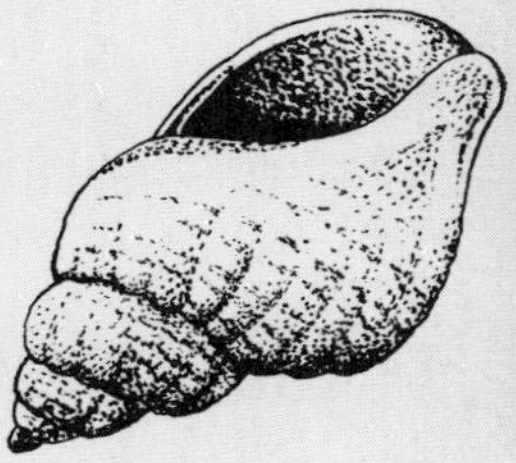
8c

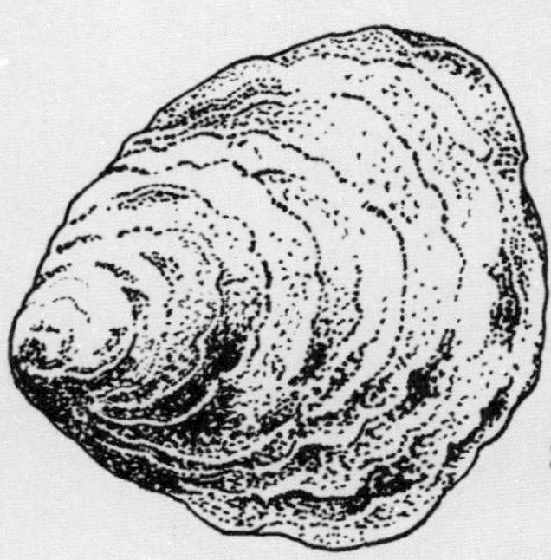
8d

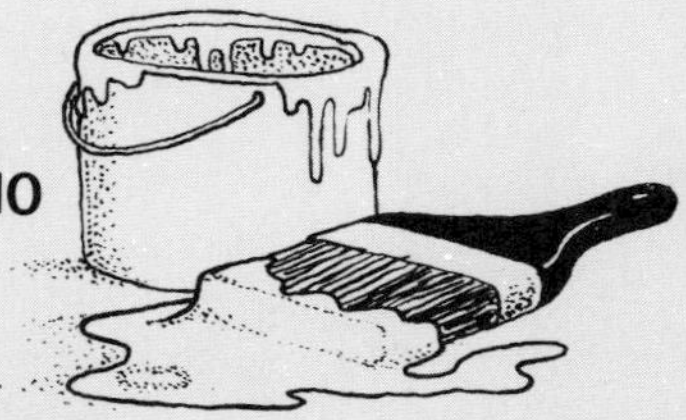
10

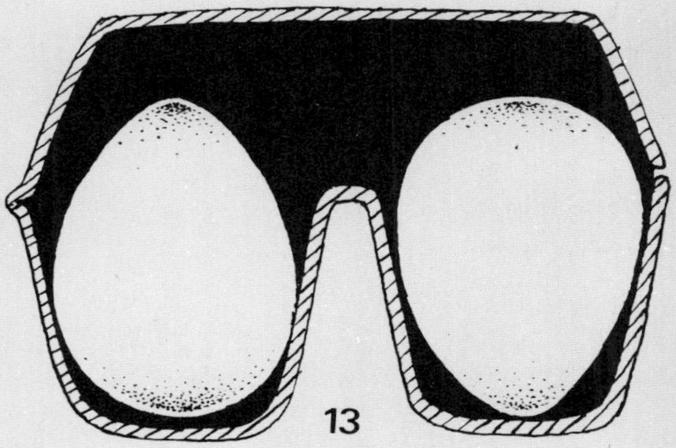
13

Answers on page 61

HAIR CARE

by Fiona Lawson

illustrated by Jil Shipley

How would you describe your hair—your crowning glory, or a messy thatch of split ends? Lovely hair will give you confidence in yourself and makes an excellent first impression, so it is worth taking the extra time and trouble to care for it properly. Want to know more? Hair goes!

WHAT IS HAIR?

The roots of the hair, growing under the scalp, are a living part of your body, just as the skin and blood are. The roots are made of a type of protein known as keratin, and each individual hair starts off as a tiny bud called a medulla which, like all the other parts of the body, needs to be fed properly to grow well. So if you want shiny, healthy hair, you must start from the inside by feeding it properly. This means concentrating on fresh foods like fruit and vegetables and cutting down on 'junk' foods like sweets, crisps and fizzy drinks. Don't feel that you must give them up completely—but there's no doubt that too many of these foods will make you unhealthy. Your skin will suffer and so will your hair—it will be dull and lifeless and will probably have dandruff too. *Yuk!* So the message is clear—healthy hair starts from within. Get into the habit of eating properly and your hair will respond by looking better and better.

The average adult head contains around 120,000 hairs, each of which has a life cycle of about three years. However, don't worry if some of the hairs on your head don't seem to want to live that long! Most of us lose 80-90 hairs each day, more if we use a brush and comb frequently and the normal growth rate for hair is between ½'' and ¾'' a month.

Hair is amazingly elastic stuff and can put up with quite a lot of wear and tear without protest. But that shouldn't give you free licence to treat it as if it were old rope! The more care you take with it, the better your hair will look. There's no magic formula, just find the right routine for you and follow it. The basic steps are:

WASHING

Basically, you should use a shampoo to suit your hair type: normal, dry, or greasy. The best shampoo may not be the most expensive one, so don't be afraid to use the cheaper brands. There are also shampoos for special problems, such as dandruff.

Wash your hair as often as it seems to need it; you may find that it sometimes needs washing more often than usual, for instance during a hot spell, or when you have your period.

How to wash your hair is just as important as when. A lot of people make the mistake of using too much shampoo and then not rinsing properly. The correct amount to use is a dollop on your hand the size of a 10p piece—no larger. Wet the hair, then apply the shampoo by adding a little water to the shampoo on your hand and rubbing your hands together. Spread this mixture over all your hair, wash gently but thoroughly, rinse and repeat the process. If you have very greasy hair try to be as gentle as possible as too much rubbing of the scalp will activate the oil glands and make the problem worse. Whatever your hair type, never have the water more than hand hot—remember, the scalp is sensitive. Also, ***always*** wash your brushes and combs at the same time, or you will end up with dirty hair again in no time. After the second washing, rinse, rinse, and rinse again! It's essential to remove every particle of shampoo, or your hair will look dull and lifeless. A shower spray is much better for this job, so invest in one if you can; (Boots sell a range of inexpensive ones).

One last point about shampoos. Always check the label for special instructions, particularly if you are using a 'treatment' shampoo.

CONDITIONING

The hair has its own natural 'conditioner'—sebum oil, which helps to keep it in good condition. Constant washing and drying tend to strip away this natural oil, so it is a very good idea to use a conditioner. It will make the hair softer, less tangled and easier to brush and comb, which in turn means that it will be less prone to split ends. Which type to choose? Again, choose one to suit your hair type. There are all kinds available, including oil-free ones for greasy hair—yes, greasy hair ***does*** need a conditioner! Do read the instructions carefully before you start, and do rinse ***very*** thoroughly.

If you are short of money and/or there is no conditioner in the house, you can make your own from one simple ingredient—an egg! For greasy hair, lightly beat the ***white*** with a squeeze of lemon juice. Apply to the hair, leave on for 1-2 minutes and rinse off. For normal to dry hair, add a drop of water to the ***yolk*** to thin it out and apply this to your hair, leaving it on for 3-4 minutes. Rinse well with ***tepid*** water—any hotter and you may end up with a head full of scrambled egg!

DRYING

The best way to dry hair is to let it dry naturally, but this can take so long, especially with thick or long hair, that most people use a blow drier. Be warned, however—blow drying aggravates any tendency to split ends, so bear this in mind if you have naturally weak hair. If you *must* blow dry, remember the three main rules:

i. Always use a conditioner first to protect the hair.

ii. Set the hair drier to warm—never hot.

iii. Always use the drier so that it is facing down the length of your hair, not up towards your scalp.

If your hair tends to split when blow dried but looks awful if left to dry naturally why not think about using rollers to set it? Steer clear of the spiky, plastic kind, and go for the jumbo-sized foam rollers which give a bouncy, natural curl.

PROBLEM HAIR

The two most common problems with young hair are dandruff and split ends. Both are unsightly, but perfectly possible to cure, so don't despair!

Dandruff is unsightly and can be embarrassing, but there are special shampoos available which should clear up the problem.

Split ends are a result of damage to the hair and once they occur, should be cut off. It is possible however to do a great deal to prevent them reappearing. Never drag a brush or comb through wet hair, but comb it very gently with a wide-toothed comb, starting at the ends and gradually taking in longer strands, working up to the scalp. Never rub wet hair vigorously with a towel; always pat it gently. Never use elastic bands—the hair's worst enemy!—and try to have your hair trimmed about every six weeks.

HAIR STYLES

Hair fashions come and go so quickly that it would be pointless to give suggestions here. However, there are certain rules to bear in mind when choosing a new style. Some styles will suit very thick, curly hair, but not fine, straight hair, and vice versa, so do ask your hairdresser for advice. Basically, though, it's best to choose a style to suit your shape of face:

A ROUND FACE needs a style which will add a little height and create an illusion of extra length. The last thing you need is a straight fringe cutting right across your forehead, though a fine, wispy fringe would look pretty. A softly curling style which covers the ears can look very flattering, as can a diagonal effect formed by a sideways sloping fringe. Do steer clear of a cut which stops short just at jaw level—this will only draw attention to the area you want to forget about!

A SQUARE FACE can look stunning with the right style. A side parting or off-centre sloping fringe will take away from any heavy look at jaw level. Long hair looks terrific with a square face and waves are flattering. Styles to avoid are very short ones or long hair scraped back off the face.

AN OVAL FACE—lucky you! This shape of face looks good with virtually any hairstyle, even perfectly straight, long hair. Don't let that be an excuse for letting your hair get out of condition though!

A HEART-SHAPED FACE can look very pretty if it is not swamped by too much hair. Stick to a shoulder length or short look and accentuate your pointed chin by keeping the hair behind the ears if possible. Smooth, straight hair suits this shape of face, so aim for a sleek, well-groomed look.

No matter what shape your face is, your hair style should be easy to care for, should suit your way of life, and should need the minimum effort to keep it looking good. Find a hairdresser and a hair style you like, and life will be easier all round!

FUN STYLES

Once in a while it's nice to do something completely different, maybe for a party, a holiday, or an outing. There are all sorts of hair decorations available—combs, slides and so on, to brighten up the plainest style. The prettiest effect of all can be achieved by simply tucking a fresh flower or two into the hair, discreetly held in place by a clip.

If you have long, straight hair and feel like a complete change, why not try plaiting? Wash your hair, pat away the excess moisture with a soft towel and comb out carefully. Then, starting at the front of the head and gradually working round, take a thickish strand of hair and work it into a three-stranded plait. Secure the ends with a piece of cotton rag. Carry on this way until you have plaited all the way round your head. You could end up with anything from 8 to 18 plaits, depending on the thickness of your hair and the plaits. Leave the plaits in overnight if possible, and when your hair is dry, untie the rags and carefully unplait your hair. Shake your head vigorously and gently run your fingers through your hair from the scalp to the ends. Do NOT try to comb or brush it. Your hair should be a rippling mass of waves! The effect will last for a few days, but will disappear when you wash your hair, so you can be back to normal again in time for school!

JOIN THE PENCIL SET

by Phyllis Mead

illustrated by Chris Sheridan

fig. 1

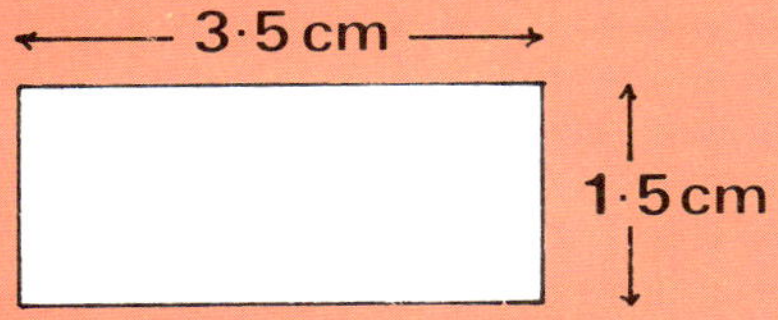

fig. 2

fig. 3

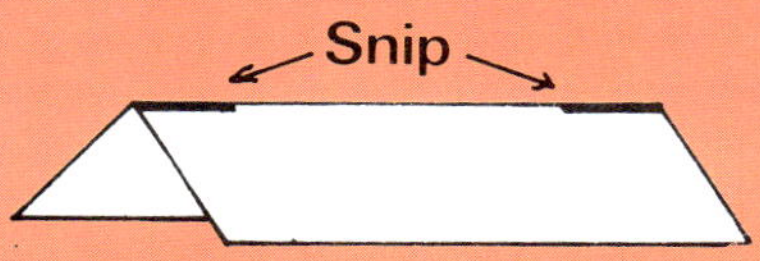

fig. 4

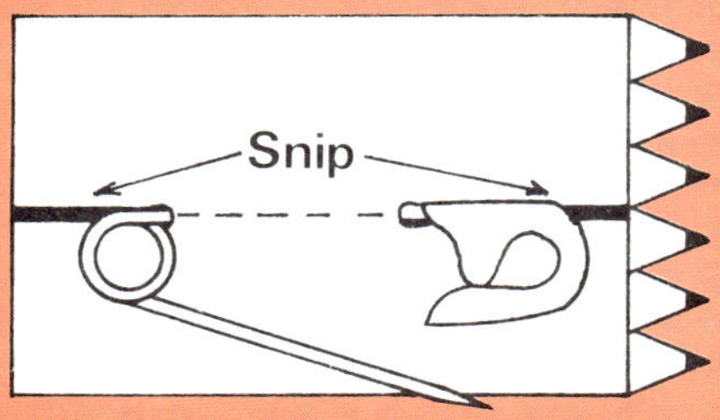

fig. 5

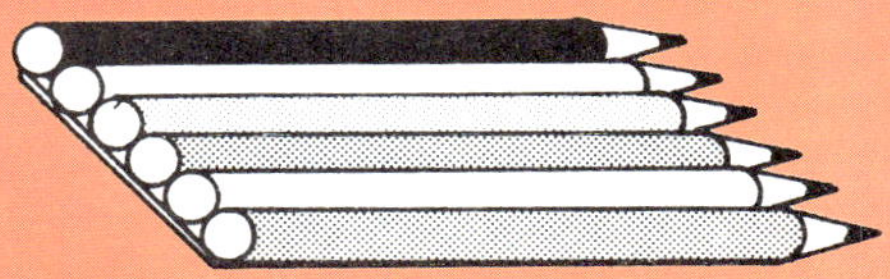

Make a super brooch!

You will need:
3 wooden cocktail sticks
scraps of thin card and felt
powder or poster paints or felt-tipped pens
polyurethane varnish
white spirit
fine sandpaper
a large safety pin
pencil, ruler, pair of scissors, sharp knife and a small paint brush
Uhu or other fabric glue

First, measure cocktail sticks and cut each one exactly in half. Sandpaper each 'pencil', taking special care to smooth the cut ends.

Colour the shaft of each 'pencil' leaving the pointed end bare apart from a tiny dab of colour on the tip (fig 1).

Cut a rectangle of card and one of felt 1.5cm × 3.5cm (fig 2).

When the 'pencils' are dry, mount them side by side on the card with their points protruding, using glue (fig 3).

Give your 'pencil set' two coats of varnish, making sure that the first coat is thoroughly dry before applying the second.

Fold the felt rectangle in half along its length.

Snip the crease at both ends until the felt lies smoothly through the safety pin (fig 4).

With the safety pin in position, glue the felt to the back of your brooch (fig 5).

Don't forget to clean your paint brush with white spirit immediately after applying each coat of varnish.

Fish from the Tropics

by Ann Pinder

illustrated by Jim Channell

Zebras in the living room? That might sound a strange, not to say inadvisable idea, but not when you're the owner of tropical fish, since this is the name of a variety of tiny black and white striped fish, very popular with aquarium owners.

The zebra fish, an inhabitant of slow moving waters and paddy fields, came originally from eastern India and is just one of a vast array of fishes now seen in aquaria but originating in exotic parts of the world like South America, Africa, Thailand and the West Indies.

Trinidad plays host to the guppy, sometimes called the millions fish, because it is so prolific, producing an average litter of up to fifty young at a time. Easy to keep, the guppy is an ideal choice for the new aquarium owner, and is particularly interesting since it produces live young, rather than eggs. But the guppy is not alone in this; several other aquarium fish are also live bearers as well as being attractive additions to the tank. These are the platy, the sword-tail, and the black and sailfin mollies, vegetarians from Mexico which feed on aquatic plants and algae and also have a liking for lettuce.

Many fish, the guppy included, will eat their young if they get the chance, so adults and fry must be kept apart until the youngsters are too big to provide a juicy mouthful. Conversely though, some fish actually protect their young by keeping them in the mouth, providing a safe harbour for the eggs, and then for the newly hatched young, which swim in and out at will. These mouth brooders belong to the cichlid family, which includes the majestic angel fish from the Amazon Basin. Though not a mouth brooder, it is a conscientious parent, guarding the eggs when they are laid on water plants, and fanning them with fresh water until they are ready to hatch, when the parents chew open the egg-shells.

Despite its name, the angel fish can be quite aggressive, as are several other species which may harrass smaller tenants of the tank, so do seek expert advice when stocking a new tank or purchasing an addition for an established tank, as not all fish can be kept together.

A case in point is the Siamese fighting fish, which will not tolerate another male in his vicinity, and will fight, sometimes with fatal results. The males are beautiful fish though, with flowing fins, and it is worth keeping a pair, to watch them making a nest, a raft of bubbles constructed by the male on the surface of the water, into which he blows the eggs as they are laid by the female.

The dwarf gourami is also a bubble-nest builder. The male is very popular, being brightly adorned in blue-grey with red stripes. For most people the main reason for keeping tropical fish is to appreciate their attractive appearance, so the zebras are very popular too, as they flash about the tank, and the neon tetras, alight with jewel bright colours, are a worthwhile addition to any tank.

But we should not ignore the less attractive tank-bottom feeders, which consume algae and waste food and help to keep the tank clean. Notable among these are the streamlined loaches, and the sinister looking catfish, so called for the whiskery projections around its mouth, used as feelers in the dark. One shy South American catfish, plecostomus, fastens itself to the underside of rocks by means of a suction disc, but emerges from this retreat to feed. It is a useful addition to the tank as it feeds on plant algae without damaging the plant, although unfortunately it will also consume angel fish eggs if it comes across them.

To avoid mistakes when starting up an aquarium do seek advice from your local aquarium shop, and read up about tropical fish and fish keeping in one of the many excellent publications now on sale, or available from your library. Then, armed with the relevant information, set about buying your tank and equipment. This will consist of a hood with lighting facilities, a pump to keep the water fresh, and a heater and thermostat to warm the water and maintain it at a constant temperature of about 24°C (75°F). Washed gravel will be required, plus a selection of aquatic plants which will not only provide shelter for shy fish, and egg-laying sites, but also help to oxygenate the water and be a source of food for vegetarian species.

Once your tank is set up allow it to mature for several days with the heater switched on. Only then, when everything has settled down and the water is at the required temperature, should you go and buy the fish. Introduce the fish gradually by floating their transportation bag on the water in the tank for a few hours, then when the water in both the bag and the tank are at the same temperature you can release the fish into their new home.

LET'S DANCE

by Penny Morris

photographs by Mary Vaughan

Sandra and Antonia begin with simple warming-up exercises

'The chance to dance and exercise for everyone' is the slogan of Dancercise, a company formed 12 years ago by Phyllis Morgan, an American who wanted to encourage people to exercise in an enjoyable way, through dance. The system uses choreographed exercises based on classical, modern and jazz dancing, with some ballet, tap and yoga movements. The aim of Dancercise is 'to give you the elegance and trim, firmness and flow of a dancer'. You follow the exercises to build a repertoire of dance steps and routines which will limber up and strengthen every part of your body.

At the moment Dancercise is only taught in and around London. Nearly all the teachers have been professional dancers, and Phyllis herself studied at the Ballet Russe and Martha Graham schools in New York, and danced in Broadway musicals.

I went along to meet Phyllis and to watch her taking a class. Most Dancercise classes are held in discotheques, using the disco lighting and sound systems, so the atmosphere is exciting. The first class I watched was for beginners and did not seem too difficult, but the second class, for intermediate students, was much faster and more strenuous. It was marvellous to see how everyone enjoyed the class, laughing as they tried and failed to follow the difficult routines! Whenever the students found a sequence rather hard, Phyllis would take them over that part again until they had grasped

The class gets going with stretching movements

Louise shows an exercise for leg muscles

it. Then the class would perform the whole routine to the music. I was very impressed by the professional appearance of the group, and the way everyone put so much energy into the exercises.

Having seen a couple of sessions, I took two Guides along to a beginners' class run by Louise Burgess, who teaches Dancercise disco-style.

The exercises build into a sequence

Antonia Gissing and Sandra Welsh, two members of 23rd Croydon Guide Company, bravely agreed to be the guinea pigs, and we went to a discotheque called Busby's in Tottenham Court Road.

Having changed into leotards, the Guides joined the other beginners on the disco floor, and for the next 75 minutes they stretched, turned and danced to the funky music, following Louise's directions.

By the end of the class it was plain that the Guides had enjoyed themselves as much as the regular Dancercisers. When they had changed and recovered their breath, I asked them what they thought. They both agreed that Dancercise was a great way to keep fit, and much more fun than most conventional types of physical education.

If you want to try the Dancercise system you can send for a cassette called 'Dancercise and all that Jazz'. The tape contains spoken instructions as well as music and takes you from warming-up movements, through fitness exercises, to a full dance routine. There are photographs to help you. Perhaps a group of you could use the tape to learn a dance routine to perform at a Guide concert? Once you've got the hang of it, you could make up your own routines for discos and parties! If you would like a Dancercise tape, write to DANCERCISE, THE BARGE DURBAN, OLD ISLEWORTH, MIDDLESEX.

The class uses Busby's disco lighting and sound system

Louise helps with a complicated sequence

The spectacular lighting helps create a really exciting atmosphere

BRASS RUBBINGS

photographs by Neil Fraser

by Fiona Lawson

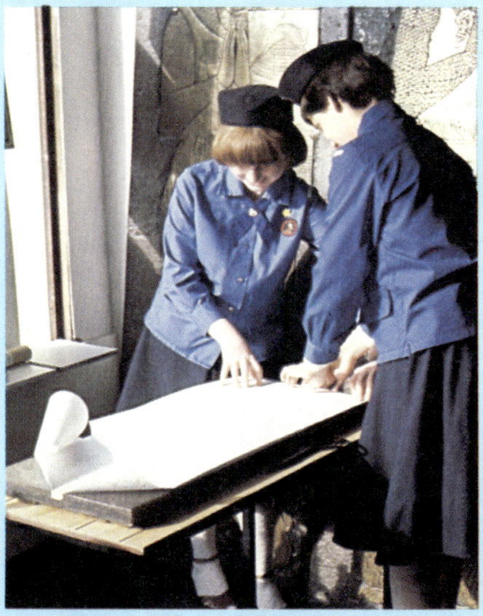

"EXPERIMENT in textural patterns, using rubbings, string prints, waste-card prints, glass prints, etc".

If you are working for your Guide Artist Badge at the moment, or are hoping to in the future, you will probably recognise the section of the badge test syllabus above. Even if you're not thinking about the badge at the moment, though, you may well find that experiments of this sort can lead you to a fascinating hobby, working with different objects to create your own pictures. Once you get involved, you'll be so fascinated by your new hobby that you'll find it difficult to give up!

Let's start with brass rubbing. To find out how it's done, we went along to the Greenwich Brass Rubbing Centre with two Guides from the 2nd Kidbrooke Company: Kay Minns, aged thirteen, and Yasamin Rowshankish, aged twelve years.

Neither of the girls had tried brass rubbing before, but they were amazed at how easy it was once they started! Gerard Gillan, the owner of the centre, explained the process to them step by step as they went along.

Step 1. Having chosen the design they liked best, the girls set to work by first covering it with thin paper, stretched very tight. The type of paper they used was 70gsm. white art paper, although they could equally well have chosen one of several other colours available.

It's very important to stretch the paper as taut as possible, otherwise it might wrinkle and distort the final rubbing. When they had done this, Yasamin and Kay stuck the paper down round the edges with lots of masking tape—Sellotape would have left sticky marks behind.

Step 2. Choosing the wax. Gerard recommended Astral Wax, a particularly hard wax made especially for brass rubbings. It is possible to use ordinary wax crayons (the kind children draw with) but being softer, they tend to smudge more and block out the details. Yasamin and Kay were surprised at the wide selection of colours they could have chosen—all sorts of shades, from silver to scarlet. Gerard told them that the metallic colours—silver, bronze and gold—can be rubbed out when used on black paper, so are the best kind for beginners. However, the Guides felt brave enough to try the black wax on white paper, which is in fact the traditional colour scheme for brass rubbings.

Step 3. The next step was to carefully feel round the outline of the figure to find its edges. The girls learned how to scratch round the rim of the figure with a fingernail so that the outline stood up in relief. Once this is done, it is easier to work within the figure and not stray over the edge. Even so, the girls found that it helped to hold a piece of card against the edge of the figure as they worked, just in case!

Step 4. Now for the hard work! Kay and Yasamin soon found that the best—and easiest—way to work was to keep stroking the wax in the same direction, using firm hand movements. As the picture appeared on the paper, they 'tidied up' areas which weren't particularly strong, and carefully drew in the delicate details of the face, etc., as the outlines appeared. The whole rubbing was completed in about ten minutes and looked very professional indeed—so good, in fact, that the girls promptly decided to try another one!

This time they used pale blue paper and black wax for a different look, although of course the technique was the same. This brass took slightly longer, being more detailed, but the end result looked just as good. Yasamin and Kay were delighted to be able to take the finished rubbings home with them. Kay was going to hang hers as a scroll on the wall, while Yasamin, who is good at needlework, planned to work an embroidered picture based on the first rubbing.

About the brasses

Brass rubbing has been popular in England for hundreds of years, starting around the middle of the thirteenth century and reaching a peak of popularity in the mid-17th century.

The first engraving Yasamin and Kay chose to work on was the well-known 'Margaret Peyton', a brass rubbing you may well have seen illustrated in books as it is a very popular one. The subject is an attractive medieval lady wearing a heavily patterned gown, probably made from rich Italian brocade, and the 'butterfly' type headdress which was very popular in the Middle Ages. The original brass came from Isleham in Cambridgeshire and dates back to 1484.

Their second choice was an engraving of 'John Chudleigh' from Hinton in Somerset, dating from around the same period. The subjects of most brasses from this period were members of the aristocracy who must have had a great deal of money for luxuries—it has been estimated that a life-size brass figure, like the ones behind the girls in the photographs, would cost between £30,000 and £40,000 today!

Brass rubbing can be a fascinating and rewarding hobby—after all, you can take the end product home with you! There are quite a few brass rubbing centres around the country, but if there isn't one near you, then try your local church. The vicar or minister will be able to tell you if there are any suitable brasses which you could work on, and show you where to find them.

You can buy suitable paper, wax, etc. to work with from artists' supply shops and craft shops, or you could ask your art teacher at school for help. If there are no suitable shops near you, you can buy items by mail order from suppliers such as Studio 69, Elm Hill, Norwich, Norfolk (telephone 40-22827). Send an s.a.e. for a price list.

Once you start brass rubbings, you will probably want to experiment with other types of rubbing too. Some of the more obvious items you could practise on are coins, manhole covers and postbox plaques—but why not take one step further and produce your own bases for the rubbings? It's really very easy and you will have the satisfaction of knowing that it is *all* your own work!

CREATIVE RUBBINGS

written and illustrated by Kathryn Baxter

The methods used for making your own designs and rubbings are very simple. While you are working on your design you can take small sample rubbings to see how the design is coming along and if any alterations are needed. Parts of the design can be taken off and placed on different parts of the background until you have arranged the whole plan as you wish.

What you will need to make the original design:

1. A pair of scissors with straight blades.
2. A non-lumpy paste, suitable for paper. The cellulose type used for wallpaper is both cheap and good.
3. A small paste brush to apply it with.
4. A piece of thin sugar paper, or similar, to use as the background onto which you will glue your design. This is available from craft shops, or perhaps your art teacher at school could help you out.

You will also need smaller pieces of paper with which to make the picture. For this you can use sugar paper, wrapping paper, magazine pages, notepaper and even envelopes! Remember, though, that if you use a strongly textured paper (such as some types of wallpaper or brown paper), its pattern will show through on your completed rubbing.

What you will need to make the rubbing:

1. Any sort of black or wax crayon. Different sorts will give different tones and qualities to the rubbing and generally speaking, the stronger and harder the crayon is, the better. Large crayons are easier to hold.
2. Paper, onto which the rubbing will be made. It should be thin, strong and smooth. Kitchen shelving paper is ideal, and is a pale buff colour which can be a pleasant change from white. Typing paper is also good, but is only available in fairly small sheets. Detail paper is very good and can be obtained from any shop which supplies architects' and draughtsmen's materials. It is thicker and stronger than shelving paper and it is white. It is available in rolls as well as in sheets.

The method

This falls into two parts—firstly the cutting and sticking to make the original, and secondly making the rubbing from your original.

1. First, take the paper which will form the background sheet of your picture. It must have straight edges. Now cut out some shapes (see diagrams) from another piece of paper. Paste the back of these cut shapes and stick them down on the background sheet. Be careful not to drip paste onto the backing sheet in the spaces between the shapes, as it will cause wrinkling and this will show up on the rubbing. The best results come from using the same colour of paper for both the backing sheet and the cut-out shapes; without the distraction of different colours one is aware of the shapes and thicknesses of the layers.

Experiment as much as possible at this stage; try out different shapes and formations by laying them down and moving them around without sticking them down. When you have made your own decision, remember to use only a small amount of paste when sticking down, as too much will cause wrinkling. Similarly, if there are too many layers of shapes the paper will wrinkle and blur the rubbing. Give the paste adequate time to dry out or the paper will curl and distort.

2. When the paste is completely dry, spread the original out flat on a table with a smooth hard surface, such as formica. If a wooden table is used the grain of the wood may show through the rubbing. The table should be clean and free from crumbs, hair, etc., as these will show on the rubbing too.

3. Smooth the rubbing paper over the original and secure the corners with masking tape (fig. 1). The tape can be removed when the rubbing is finished and will leave no mark.

The technique of rubbing is as creative as the original. Use the whole length of your crayon, not just the tip (if it has a paper covering this can easily be removed). If you rub evenly all over the design, each part will have the same emphasis. The design will show up better if some parts have a stronger tone, which is achieved by harder rubbing, and other areas lightly rubbed or left white. You can follow the direction of the forms you have made with the strokes of the crayon to enhance them. To really get the most from your rubbing, experiment with strokes and tones as much as you can. See how many ways you can find of rubbing a simple shape (fig. 2).

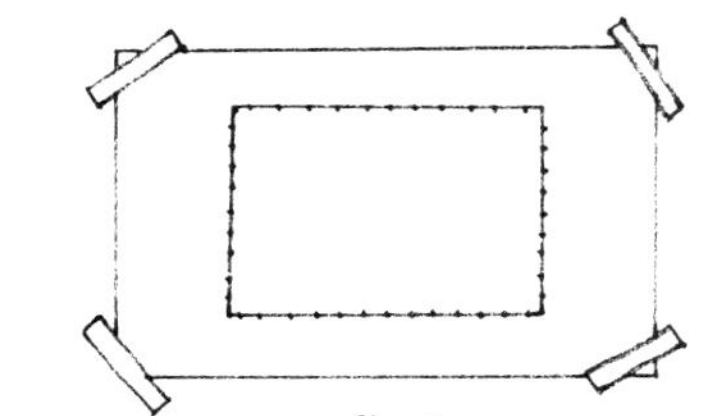
fig 1

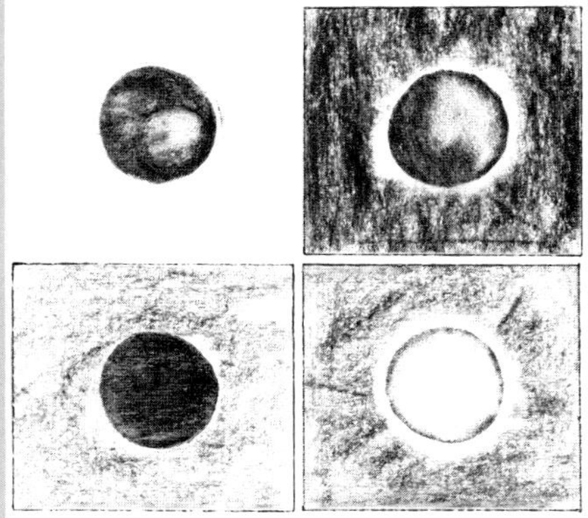
fig 2

fig 3

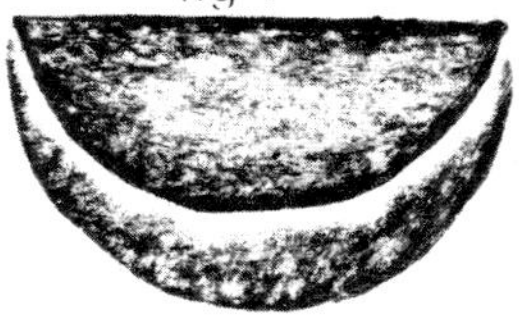
fig 4

fig 5

fig 6

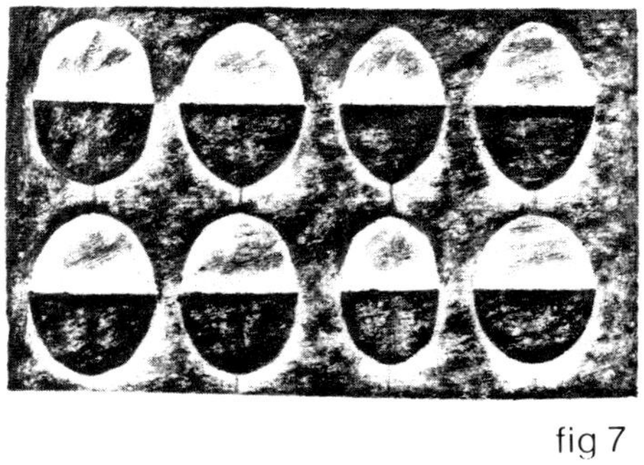
fig 7

fig 8

fig 9

fig 10

fig 11

The techniques of folding, cutting and bending

These methods of treating paper make the resulting rubbing look very three dimensional. There are four ways oı folding:

1. Use simple shapes such as squares, triangles or circles and fold over parts of them ***without*** cutting (figs. 3, 4 and 5).

2. Fold a piece of paper lengthwise. Cut into the fold, open out the paper and bend back the cut pieces (figs. 6, 7 and 8).

3. Using a very sharp cutting knife or scalpel, cut into the middle of a piece of paper and fold back the shapes. Use a board to cut on to prevent marking the table (fig. 9).

4. Cut into the edges of the paper and fold back the pieces (figs. 10 and 11).

Spreading

In the spreading technique, the shape is cut out of one piece of paper and some features are cut around it. The surrounding pieces are moved a little apart before being stuck down. There is a white line left in the gap.

Hints

If you have difficulty drawing certain shapes try cutting out pictures from magazines or comics and rubbing them, or you could copy pictures from books that you did not want to cut up. Old Christmas cards can be cut up and, using the spreading technique, new ones rubbed. The rubbings can be coloured, using inks, watercolour paints or felt tip pens.

The edges of the background paper should be rubbed cleanly as this makes a good border frame for the design. This is why edges must be straight. The same cut shape or motif can be moved about and rubbed many times on the paper to give a pattern without having to cut out many shapes which are all exactly the same. Melt down small leftover pieces of wax crayon in an old saucepan or a clean tin and pour into tinfoil or a jam jar lid to set.

GUIDE BADGE WORD SEARCH

by Phyllis Mead

Can you find all the Guide Interest Badges listed below in the letter block?

- Agility
- Backwoodsman
- Bellringer
- Be Prepared
- Camper
- Cook
- Craft
- Cyclist
- Gardener
- Hiker
- Horsewoman
- Naturalist
- Rambler
- Reader
- Skater
- Skier
- Star Gazer
- Toymaker
- Traveller

E	B	E	P	R	E	P	A	R	E	D	A	Q
J	C	A	M	P	E	R	A	M	B	L	E	R
N	R	P	C	R	E	T	T	C	C	H	S	T
O	E	F	Y	K	F	D	Y	J	R	O	F	S
R	G	Z	I	A	W	C	T	G	E	R	Y	I
E	N	H	R	T	L	O	S	A	T	S	T	L
L	I	C	L	I	Y	B	O	R	A	E	I	A
L	R	N	S	M	R	S	R	D	K	W	L	R
E	L	T	A	P	R	E	C	E	S	O	I	U
V	L	K	J	E	D	R	O	N	V	M	G	T
A	E	I	I	A	O	V	O	E	X	A	A	A
R	B	K	E	U	Y	E	K	R	D	N	C	N
T	S	R	S	T	A	R	G	A	Z	E	R	O

Solution on page 61

Makes you think

by Ann Hillyer

"Can you come and help with weeding?"
"Not now, Dad—I'm busy reading!"
"Could you do a bit of baking?"
"Sorry, Mum—my head's still aching!"
"Make this model, Sis, for me!"
"Buzz off, Ted—it's too near tea!"
Rover begs, "Oh, please play ball!"
Then the phone—Mum takes the call.
"That was Guider—weekend hike."
"Just the kind of thing I like!"
"Guider wanted you to go;
I said, 'She's too tired, I know!
Cooking, camping, life outdoors,
All of these she finds such bores.'
Jenny Smith is going instead,
So you can lounge about in bed!"

So 'Be Prepared', Guides, every one—
Or else you too may miss your fun!

A CHALLENGE FOR CLAIRE

by Ann Hillyer

illustrated by Valerie Sangster

"Heard the latest news?" Alison called to Claire as they arrived at the Guide Hut on Tuesday evening, as usual.

"You mean about the Helping Hand Scheme that the P.L.s have dreamed up?" Claire said in reply.

"No—about the Guide Hut being taken over by the supermarket next door! My dad works for the building firm which is going to convert it into a storage area. They're starting next month!"

"But what about us?" Claire wanted to know. She was one of the keenest Guides in the 3rd Norchester Company. "There's nowhere else on this estate where we can meet."

They found the Guider talking to a Brownie Leader, whose girls also used the Guide Hut during the week.

"Now, whilst I am discussing what we can do about finding another meeting-place with Mrs Jackson," began Skipper, shushing the eager voices around her, "Helen will tell you what we've decided in P.L. Council about the annual Helping Hand Scheme."

Helen was a tall, confident girl, well liked by the others. "As you know, there are only twelve of us in this Company," said Helen. "We chatted about the best way in which we could help the people on this estate who most need it—and in the end Lorraine had the best idea."

"It was really my mum's idea," broke in Lorraine. Her mother was a health visitor.

"There are several elderly people living alone," Helen went on, "in fact we were able to make a list of twelve names. People who have difficulty getting around, or coping with household jobs—that sort of thing. More important—people whose families don't live near enough to pop in regularly."

"So we've got to 'adopt' an old person and look after them a bit," said Claire. "That sounds easy enough."

"I could cook them a dinner and whizz round with it on my roller-skates!" chimed in Alison, who was always full of fun. "Then I could say I was Meals on Wheels!"

"You would!" laughed Skipper, coming over. "But although Claire said it sounds easy, don't forget that some old people get a bit tired and grumpy—and some are very independent. Now then, Helen's written all the names and addresses on bits of paper, and I want you to draw one out of the bag. That's the fairest way!"

"Mrs Marshall!" cried Alison, dipping in first. "Oh, super! She makes that delicious fudge for the bazaar each Christmas. Hope she gives me some when I call on her!"

"You'll be calling in every day, and you'll end up getting fat!" teased Lorraine. "Oh look—I've got Mr West. He's a sweet old man! I haven't got a grandad, so it will be nice to have an 'adopted' one."

"Who have you got, Claire?" asked Alison.

Claire unfolded the paper. "Miss Fowler," she said quietly.

The girls looked at each other. Miss Fowler was slightly lame, and lived in a large, gloomy house on the edge of the estate. The garden had once been beautiful, but now it was unkempt and rather sinister. It was well known that Miss Fowler didn't approve of young people. She had never wanted the estate to be built in the first place. She had complained about the youth club, the children on bicycles and even about the Guides who'd gone carol-singing at Christmas. She'd said they'd giggled and rung the bell too many times, and she refused to give them anything.

"Oh well, it's a challenge," decided Claire, squaring her shoulders. "The weather's warmer than it was at Christmas, so perhaps Miss Fowler will have thawed out, too!"

But she hadn't. The first time Claire called, the old lady ordered her to wipe her shoes for several minutes before allowing her in.

"Girls are slovenly nowadays!" she barked, tapping her silver-headed cane impatiently. "No point wearing a uniform if you ruin the effect with filthy shoes. Don't know why you're doing this, anyway. Can't stand charity!"

"But it's not for charity," said Claire nervously, stepping into the chilly hall hung with large portraits. "It's—well, just for friendship. I could shop for you, or read to you—or just chat, if you like!"

"Nonsense!" retorted Miss Fowler, leading her into an old-fashioned kitchen. "I order all my shopping by telephone, and I can read perfectly well without spectacles. As for chatting—I'm sure we've nothing in common. But if you really want to help, you can set to and clean this brass!"

To Claire's dismay, a large assortment of brass ornaments was spread over the big wooden kitchen table.

"Er—yes, of course," stammered Claire. "Er—do you think you could lend me an apron, or something? I don't want to get my uniform dirty."

"Well, really!" gasped Miss Fowler. "You'll be wanting me to do the job myself next, I suppose!" She took a linen tea towel from a drawer. "There—tuck that round your middle and get on with it. I've no time to waste!" And the old lady stalked out of the room, hardly using the silver-topped cane.

At the next meeting the girls were eagerly swapping stories of the old folk they'd visited. Alison had got on like a house on fire with Mrs Marshall. "She's teaching me how to crochet!" she said excitedly. "And she's asked her grand-daughter in Australia to write to me. I've always wanted a pen-friend."

"How did you get on with Miss Fowler, Claire?" asked Lorraine.

"I didn't," Claire replied gloomily. "I can't clean my shoes properly, I can't clean brass properly, and yesterday when I called, I interrupted her radio programme! Honestly, I thought she was going to hit me with that stick of hers!"

"Keep trying, Claire," encouraged Skipper. "I know Miss Fowler isn't the easiest of old ladies—but I'm sure she needs company just as much as anyone else."

"She's pretty good at disguising it, then," muttered Claire to Lorraine. "I'd swap her for your old Mr West any day!"

"He taught me some card tricks!" laughed Lorraine. "I did some ironing for him, because he's got rheumatism in his fingers—but he's still jolly nifty at card tricks, all the same!"

As the weeks went by, the Guides all made firm friends with their elderly folk. All, that is, except Claire. She still called regularly at Miss Fowler's, but either there would be a dull bit of housework to be done, or else Miss Fowler would dismiss her with a curt, "No—nothing today," as though she was selling something, Claire thought rather bitterly.

One Friday afternoon, Claire and Alison were walking home from school together.

"What a week!" puffed Alison. "Two maths tests, and extra English prep because I lost last week's, and the netball match was cancelled!"

"Well, never mind, it's the weekend now," said Claire. "Come home with me and listen to my new cassette—that folk music one. Mum won't mind."

"Aren't you going to Miss Fowler's?" Alison asked. "You did say you were."

"Oh, blow!" muttered Claire. "No—I don't think I'll bother. I did tell her I was going to call on Friday, but I don't think there's much point. She never seems very pleased to see me when I *do* go!"

They spent a happy half hour listening to the folk music. Then Alison prepared to go.

"You know, I think I will go and call on Miss Fowler after all," said Claire suddenly. "After all—it was a sort of promise, so I ought to keep it."

She walked up the overgrown path to the lonely house, and rang the doorbell. Then she rang again.

There was no answer, and no sound of Miss Fowler tapping her way down the hall with her cane.

"Good! She's out!" thought Claire, pleased, and was just about to turn and go when she thought she heard a slight sound.

A thick curtain hung behind the front door, so there was no way of seeing into the hall through the letter-box. Claire glanced at the front windows. They were all tightly shut. She heard another sound, like a groan.

"I'll try the back door," she thought, racing round. This was firmly locked, too, but one of the sash windows was slightly open.

"Thank goodness!" gasped Claire, hauling herself up on to the sill and pushing down the window to climb in.

"Who ... who's there?" called a weak voice from the hall, and Claire rushed in to find Miss Fowler lying awkwardly at the foot of the stairs.

"It's me—Claire—your Guide, remember?" explained Claire gently, for the old lady seemed confused. "Don't worry—I'll soon get help!"

"Trying to clean the stairs," murmured Miss Fowler. "Place is in such a mess—gets harder to look after it!"

Claire dialled 999 on the old-fashioned wall phone, and while they waited for the ambulance she kept up a flow of cheerful conversation to take Miss Fowler's mind off her pain.

"I'll lock up your house safely, and give the key to our Guider," she promised, "and if you have to stay in hospital, I'll visit you—if you'd like me to."

Claire was as good as her word. Miss Fowler had broken her leg, and had to stay in hospital for some time. The old lady still didn't have much to say to Claire, but she seemed pleased to see her young visitor and listened keenly as Claire told her the news.

"The other Guides and I have been working on a surprise for you when you come home," she smiled. "We've all got plenty of spare time at the moment, because our Guide Hut's been closed, and we've nowhere to meet."

When at last Miss Fowler was well enough to leave hospital, Skipper and Claire were at the house to welcome her back and hand over her key.

"It's been very good of you to keep an eye on the house for me," Miss Fowler said stiffly, opening the door.

"We've done more than that, Miss Fowler," smiled the Guider. "Claire here told us how worried you were about your housework piling up—so the Guides rallied round and tackled it for you!"

Miss Fowler gazed around in wonder. The furniture gleamed; the brass ornaments shone. The carpets had been vacuumed, and the whole house smelt clean and fresh. In the kitchen, a tempting tea was set out daintily on a tray.

"I don't know what to say..." faltered the old lady. "I've lived alone so long, I've forgotton how to make friends with people—but this young lady was determined to make friends with *me!*" And to Claire's astonishment she gave her a hug.

"I've heard all about the Guides losing their meeting place," Miss Fowler went on, going to the back window, "and I think I can do something about that. Do you see that shed down there?"

She pointed to where a large wooden building stood, surrounded by nettles. It looked shabby, but the roof was sound and it had large windows. "I want you to have it," announced the old lady. "You could soon put it to rights, I'm sure!"

Claire was sure, too.

"Well, Claire," said Skipper as they made their way home, "you started out by giving a helping hand to someone who didn't really want it—and you've ended up by helping all the Guides in the Company! And now the next challenge is—that shed!"

"It won't be as hard as Miss Fowler!" grinned Claire. "Let's make a start this Saturday!"

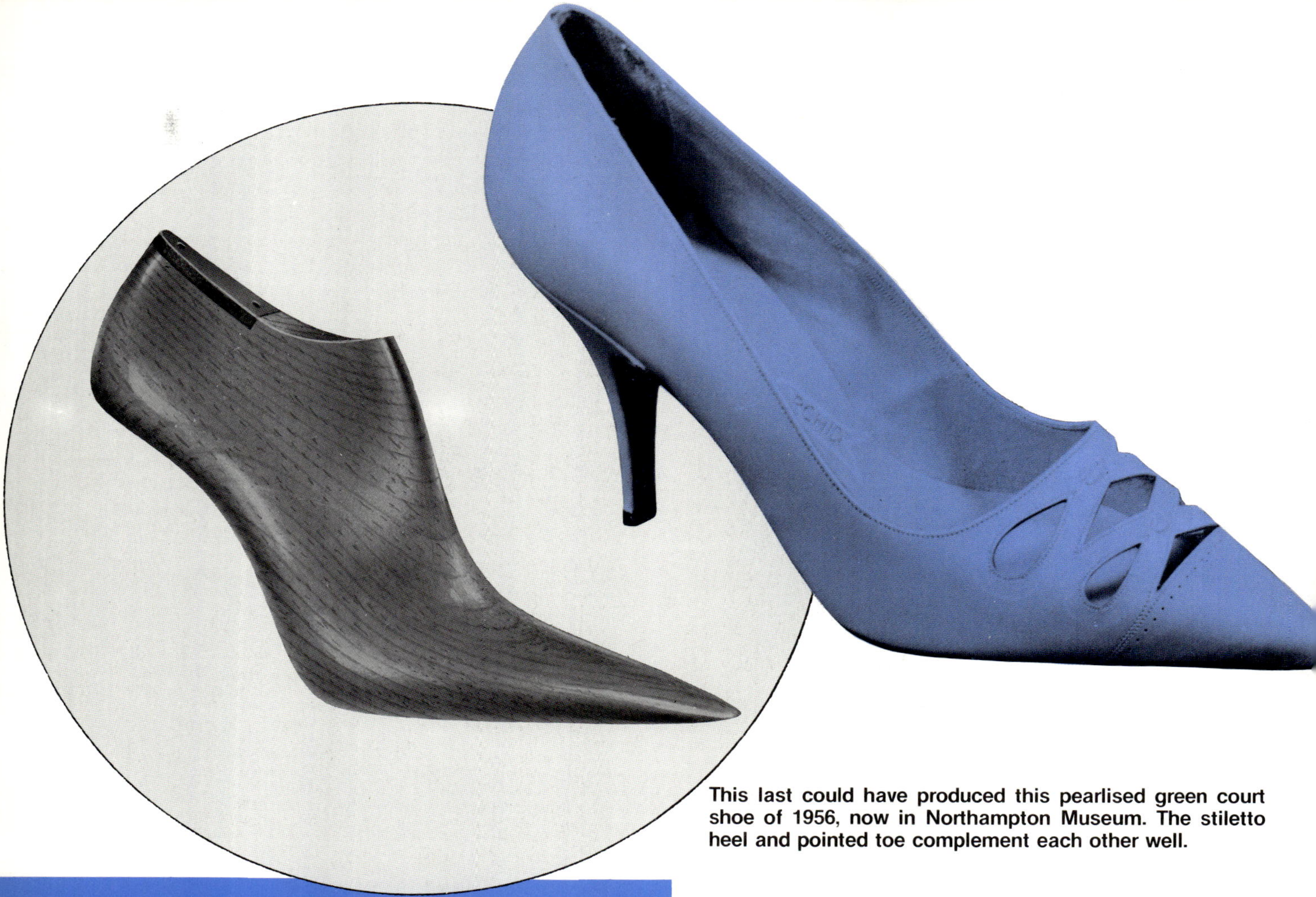

This last could have produced this pearlised green court shoe of 1956, now in Northampton Museum. The stiletto heel and pointed toe complement each other well.

The Gentle Craft

by Cecilia Fellner

Have you ever wondered how something as complicated as a shoe is designed and manufactured to fit you and perform its specific function? Shoe design and production demand highly specialised skills and training.

Examine your feet and you will appreciate how much more difficult they must be to cover than the rest of you. Basically they are wedge-shaped but all those fine bones are controlled by muscles which contract to change the shape again and again, depending on whether you are standing on tip-toe, strolling along, or carrying a heavy suitcase. Look at your friends' feet and see how individual they all are—is it any wonder that we can't all wear the same styles?

Believe it or not, it all starts with the 'last'! Shoes are designed on, and then made on, wooden or plastic lasts. Pairs of lasts come in all sizes and are roughly foot-shaped, but their basic characteristics are the result of years of experience and the actual relationship between the last, the foot and the shoe has never been scientifically formulated.

The toe-shapes of lasts vary according to fashion; so does the pitch—that is, the height of heel the last is designed to accommodate.

The designer sticks white canvas over his last and draws his design on it. Then he carefully removes the fabric without stretching it and cuts out the sections. These form the basic pieces of the pattern, though he will make adjustments later.

The shoe is cut out in leather, or whatever has been selected, in the clicking room, by a clicker—probably using a clicking knife! The blade has a sharp hook on the end. The clicker tries to use as much of the hide as he

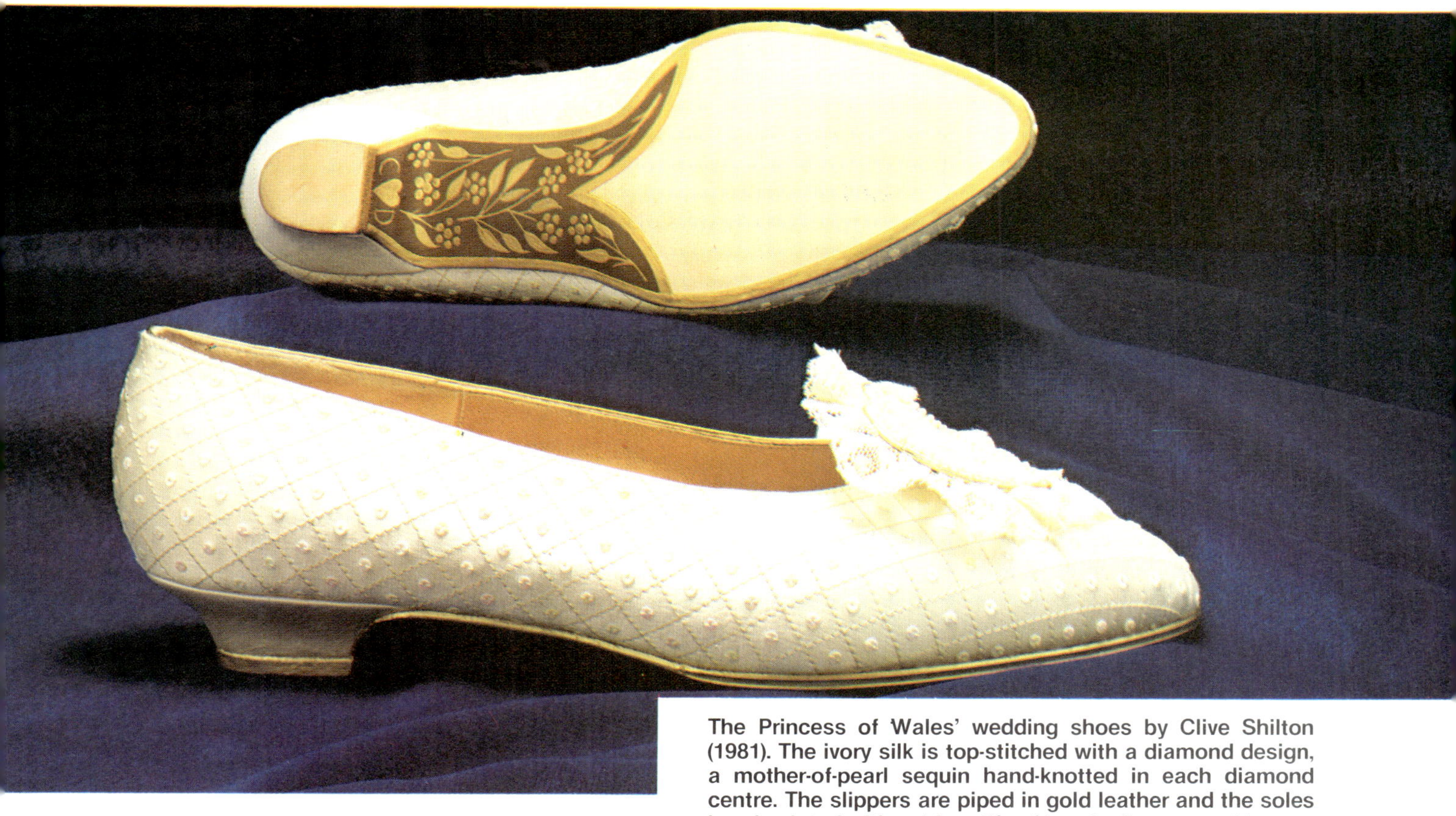

The Princess of Wales' wedding shoes by Clive Shilton (1981). The ivory silk is top-stitched with a diamond design, a mother-of-pearl sequin hand-knotted in each diamond centre. The slippers are piped in gold leather and the soles hand-painted with gold motifs of hearts, flowers and leaves. (Photograph by Theo Bergström)

can, selecting the best bits for the parts that will show most. He knows a lot about leather, which areas are likely to be strong and which stretch. He'll need both in different parts of the shoe.

The various pieces now go to the closing room where the machinists sit behind large industrial sewing machines and stitch the upper together, lining and all, using a variety of stitches.

Now back to the last! An insole is nailed temporarily onto the bottom of the last and then the assembled upper is eased over the last, avoiding any pleating over the toe, and tacked down all round the insole. Steam is a vital aid in this process. Most shoes are now machine lasted, in which case the operator has to be sure to feed the correct sections into the grippers and keep the last at the correct angle for all to go smoothly. Today's strong adhesives have done away with tacks in some designs, and some machinery moulds the sole and heel out of rubber, or some other molten resin, at the same time. More traditionally the sole and later the heel are knocked on when the last has played its part in shaping the shoe. Once removed, so-called socks, sometimes padded for comfort, are inserted inside, ornaments may be added and trimming, polishing and burnishing may be needed. Then the shoes are inspected and packed.

Every bit of this, labour and materials, has to be costed beforehand and a budget kept to for the shoes to be marketed at the price originally decided on: that is, what the sales manager estimates you will be prepared to pay. Only on rare occasions can this aspect be ignored. Clive Shilton was offered a fantastic opportunity to exercise his skills by designing and making by hand the wedding shoes for Prince Charles' bride.

Before completing the shoes, he presented to Lady Diana five different rosette designs and she chose the heartshaped design trimmed with ruffled lace and pearls.

If you feel inspired to make yourself a pair of soft shoes, why not buy one of the moccasin kits available in toy and needlework shops? You could decorate them with beads, or paint on a pattern of your own—then send us a picture of the result!

Queen Victoria's wedding shoes (1840) now in Northampton Museum.

UP TO RANGERS

by Fiona Lawson

Photographs: Chris Sheridan

Will you be leaving Guides soon because you are nearly fourteen and you have completed the Guide programme? Sad, isn't it?

Leaving Guides is no reason to leave Guiding altogether, though. More and more ex-Guides—and some girls who have never been Guides at all—are joining Rangers, and loving every minute of it.

One of the nicest aspects of Ranger Guiding is that there is no set programme to follow. Although there is a Promise Ceremony, and there are badges to work for, Ranger Units are entirely self governing and belong to their own members.

To find out what all this means when applied to a real Ranger Unit, I went along to Gravesend in Kent to visit the Thames Division Rangers. They were all very keen to talk about themselves and what they do, and equally keen to point out that, as all Units are different, they couldn't really be said to be typical in any respect!

"We're all aged around seventeen just now," said Della Platt, "but of course you can join Rangers any time after you're fourteen. Most girls leave when they're eighteen and going away to work or college, but of course there's no need to leave your Ranger Unit if you're lucky enough to be working or studying near home for a year or so."

"I'm going on to college next year," added her friend Linda Waugh. "I shall have to leave Rangers then as I'm going to a college up north, but I'm really grateful for all the things I've learned through Rangers. Yes, we have a lot of fun, but basically it's a preparation for adult life—accepting responsibility for things and learning to help others."

All the girls agreed with Linda that Ranger Guiding helps build a sense of responsibility. "We make up our own syllabus of events," Joanne Wilby told me, "so we all have an equal say in what we want to do. We find this system works very well."

"Yes," added Linda enthusiastically, "we try to make up a syllabus of events to last around four months at a time and we have a meeting once a week. Although," she continued, "Rangers don't necessarily have to meet once a week as we do. It's entirely up to each Unit to decide how often they'll meet."

"There are fourteen members in our Unit," Diane Scott told me, "but a Unit can have anything from five to twenty members, aged from fourteen to eighteen years. Our Unit had only six members when we started up two years ago, but we've built up the numbers since then. Word must have been getting round about us!"

I asked the Ranger Guider, Jane Montague, why she thought Rangers were so popular. "I think the girls appreciate being treated as adults," she told me. "By that age they're thinking things out for themselves, and I let them work out what sort of things they want to do. I never know what they're going to think up next!" she laughed.

Lydia Stephens, another member of Thames Rangers, told me about the events they had planned recently. She showed me a copy of their syllabus for that Spring—here's a section of it, decided upon after consultation with every Ranger in the Unit:

February 10th—	First Aid practice
February 14th—	Thinking Day Service in Westminster Abbey
February 17th—	Raftmaking
February 24th—	'Call My Bluff' quiz
March 3rd—	Pancake evening
March 10th—	'Managing Money'—talk by a local bank manager
March 17th—	Designing a poster to advertise Thames Rangers
March 24th—	Helping at local fête
March 31st—	Paper sculpture
April 7th—	Consumer testing report on convenience foods
April 14th—	Home maintenance: changing plugs, etc.

And that's only a sample of their activities! It certainly sounds as if the Thames Rangers have a varied programme. But what about that favourite activity of all Guides—camping? Does joining Rangers mean giving up the joys of camping?

"Not at all," said Barbara Mercer. "In fact, we're off to a four-day camp at Buckmore Park later this Spring. Why don't you come along to visit us and find out what a Ranger camp is like?"

So I did! On a warm, sunny Spring day I set off for Buckmore Park, which is a Scout-owned Camping Centre situated near Maidstone in Kent. Although owned by the Scouts, it is used by Guides, Rangers and Venture

Scouts, as well as a large contingent of overseas visitors, for camping holidays.

As I walked through the entrance gates of Buckmore Park, I recognised the Thames Rangers straight away. They were wearing very distinctive blue sweatshirts decorated with 'Thames Rangers' and their logo, a colourful sign representing the five Districts within the Division to which the Unit belongs.

I was immediately surrounded by a chattering group of Rangers who first of all took me up to "F 17", their allocated camp site. When I saw the tents pitched in a sunny little glade surrounded by trees, I remarked on how peaceful the setting looked. Julie Mercer, Barbara's sister, laughed cheerfully at this idea. "It may look peaceful now," she told me, "but you should have been here last night! We had just settled down for the night when we were disturbed by a group of ***people***,"—here Julie glared meaningfully at a group of passing Scouts—"trying to loosen our tent pegs as a joke! We had the last laugh, though, because we'd put the pegs in so securely that our midnight visitors had to give up in disgust!"

Just as Rangers are different from Guides, so Ranger camps are different from Guide camps—as I soon found out. As there are generally only a few Rangers camping together, there is no Patrol system for doing the chores, and the emphasis is on everyone lending a hand and on "organised informality", as Julie put it. After a delicious camp lunch, prepared, cooked and cleaned up by everyone, the Thames Rangers took me along to the army-style assault course which is a favourite among the amenities offered at Buckmore Park. In six minutes, they had jumped off high walls, clambered up ropes, scrambled through tunnels, scaled a 12 foot wall and walked across a wire rope. I was exhausted just watching them!

Then, only just pausing for breath, they were off again—this time to construct a wooden 'A' frame to help make a wooden monkey bridge. The logs proved a little long and heavy even for the assembled Rangers to carry, so they enlisted the help of some passing Scouts—yes, the same Scouts!—to transport the wood back to the Ranger base. In no time at all the 'A' frame was assembled and all the girls were taking turns at walking the frame. We were all amused to see that none of the Scouts was very successful!

I asked Lydia what else the Rangers intended to do while they were at Buckmore Park. "Oh, not much," she assured me, "we might go swimming later this afternoon, and roller skating, and have a go at the abseiling wall—oh, and there's the skateboarding course... and we ***did*** plan to have an overnight walk one night..."

The Thames Rangers are obviously no strangers to energetic holidays. "I think," said Della, "that being allowed to do more or less as we please encourages us to do as much as we possibly can. We're a very 'outdoor' Unit and go camping or at least hiking whenever we can, but some Units place less emphasis on being outdoors and more on other things. It all depends on how the Rangers themselves feel."

And that remark seems to sum up the general concept of Ranger Guiding—that it's run by the members, for the members, doing what ***they*** have decided to do and having a lot of fun along the way. Still feeling sad about leaving Guides?

TREES, TREES, TREES

by Penny Morris

illustrated by David More

If you are working towards the Woodcraft Emblem, you may have decided to take your Woodman's Badge. Learning to recognise different trees can be a fascinating and rewarding hobby. Here is a selection of ten of the most common.

COMMON BEECH—fagus sylvatica

This tree flowers in May, and the nuts ripen in September or October. The tree may grow to 30m and the trunk may be over 2.5m thick.

SILVER BIRCH—betula pendula

This tree is often planted in forestry plantations to protect other young trees. The catkins open in late March or April. Birches reach about 18m.

COMMON ASH—fraxinus excelsior

The ash flowers in April, and the winged seed carriers remain until the leaves have fallen. A mature ash can be up to 42m tall.

ENGLISH OAK—quercus robur

This tree is extremely long-lived, surviving up to 800 years. The flowers appear in May, and the acorns fall in October. A mature oak can be over 30m tall.

HAWTHORN—crataegus monogyna

This tree is often known as the May tree. It flowers in mid May and the fruit ripens in September. It grows to about 10m.

LOMBARDY POPLAR—populus nigra

This tree was originally from Italy. It grows up to 30m, and has a very distinctive shape. The flowers appear in March and April.

This tree flowers in April and the fruits, well known for their spiralling action, ripen in October. These trees grow to 30m tall.

SYCAMORE—acer pseudoplatanus

LONDON PLANE—platanus acerfolia

This tree grows to 30m. The flowers appear in May and the fruits develop into round green balls. The leaves can vary even on the same tree.

LABURNUM—laburnum anagyroides

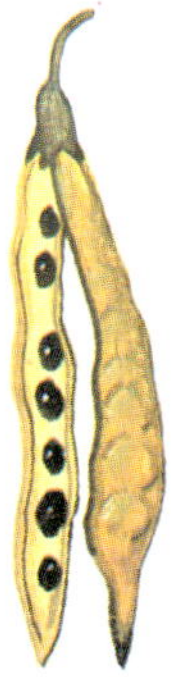

This tree's flowers, which open in May, are a rich bright yellow. The seed pods, which look like miniature pea-pods, are poisonous. It is usually 6—9m tall.

HORSE CHESTNUT—aesculus hippocastanum

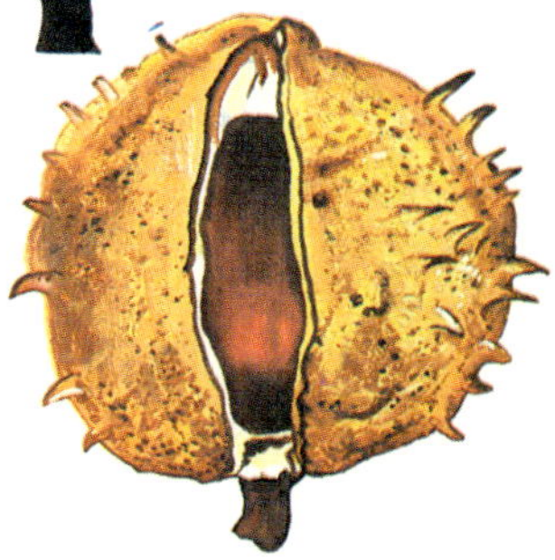

The horse chestnut's flower clusters are pink or white, and in autumn the shiny brown conkers ripen. The trees grow up to 30m.

SNAP HAPPY

by Peter Sutherst

Have you got a camera? If not, the chances are someone in your family owns one, which you can use. But for what? Let's look at some things you can do with a camera.

Remember when?

One of the best ways of using a camera is to record events, such as birthdays or holidays. Then there are new arrivals—not just a new baby but also a new bike or dress. Other memories include camping activities, award ceremonies, sports or the annual fete.

Then there are the people you meet: family, relatives, friends, colleagues, your Patrol Leader, Guide Captain or Camp Leader. You may even meet a local dignitary like the mayor. They are all worth photographing.

Equipment and Film

Cameras come in all shapes and sizes. Some, such as the KODAK 'Ektra' 200 Camera, are quite simple to use—it's just a question of point and shoot. Others are more complicated. You can get an idea of *how* complicated by the size of the instruction book!

Whichever camera you use, make sure you know how it works before you go on picture-taking expeditions. All cameras have a lens, a shutter release and a device for winding on to the next picture. More complicated models may have a focusing adjustment for the lens and perhaps variable shutter speeds and lens openings as well.

These days, many cameras have built-in flash. One of them, the KODAK 'Tele-Ektralite' 600 Camera has a built-in flash unit that thinks for itself, switching on when it gets too dark for ordinary pictures.

When it comes to using your camera, practice so that you can hold it steady. Camera movement is the number-one cause of poor pictures. Indeed, the word SNAP! gives the wrong idea when it comes to taking pictures. What you should do is gently s-q-u-e-e-z-e the shutter release, and you will be rewarded with movement free, sharp pictures. Choice of film is a question of deciding what sort of pictures you want. Most people prefer a film such as KODACOLOR II, intended for colour prints, but there are also films for slides and black-and-white prints.

BACKGROUND

Before you take your picture, look at the background. Are there any distracting elements such as light fittings, telegraph poles or trees that seem to be growing out of your subject's head? If there are, move your position. Try to choose an uncluttered background, such as the sky, so that your subject is the main element in the photograph.

Lighting is also important. Indoors, you can use flash or even the light from a nearby window. Out of doors, there is often a tendency to take your subject squinting into bright sunshine. Few people look their best with such a pained expression on their faces, so move them to a more shaded position or get them to turn so that the sun is not shining directly into their eyes.

For pictures of young children, get down to their level. This lower viewpoint will give your small subjects a more important place in their surroundings. Another trick is to move in close—but not closer than your camera will allow! Head and shoulder portraits are great for showing individual personalities. Some cameras have tele lenses that allow you to take close-ups without actually getting too close.

PEOPLE

People feature in something like 8 out of every 10 pictures taken, so how to get good pictures of people is obviously important. It all comes down to getting them to act naturally or taking them when they are not aware of you. How often have you heard people say, 'Stand over there while I take your photograph, and for goodness sake SMILE'? This type of photograph can look very artificial.

What you need for really interesting pictures is ACTIVITY. Invent an activity if necessary, but an activity that occurs naturally is best. At home, take your brothers, sisters or friends when they are playing. At camp, there are many activities. Pitching the tent usually means 'all hands on deck', but you may be able to take a few minutes off to record the action. Cooking your first meal out of doors is another event well worth catching on film. Try to get the cook intent on what she is doing rather than standing stiffly waiting for you to squeeze the shutter release.

ANIMALS

Pictures of animals involve much the same approach as pictures of people, but there are a few points to remember. Like young children, you will need to get down to the level of small animals to prevent them being lost amongst the furniture or long grass! Try to invent some activity for them. Chasing a ball of wool, chewing a slipper or drinking milk out of a saucer will keep a puppy or kitten interested for a time. But remember that their attention will soon wander. Patience is more important than picture-taking ability when it comes to photographing animals.

VIEWS

Showing the places you have visited is another plus for photography. Imagine trying to describe the view from the top of the Empire State Building! A picture not only does the job quicker but is also much more accurate. Many views don't look quite as exciting in a photograph as they do in reality. There are various complicated reasons for this, but there is one way to improve your view pictures quite easily. Use some kind of foreground object to 'frame' your view. Tree branches, the arch of a bridge, or a portion of fence will all help to give a sense of depth or scale to your photograph. Incidentally, all cameras can take excellent sunsets up to about 20 minutes before the sun actually sets. Again, include some foreground object with an interesting silhouette such as a tree or statue to give the picture depth.

USING FLASH

When the sun does go down, don't put away your camera. Activities don't stop when it's dark and you can photograph these events quite simply by using flash. There is just one restriction—you need to keep within the recommended flash distance, usually from 4 to 10 feet.

Activities at home, evening events at camp and parties are all fun to photograph. Just remember the background. Unless your friend makes a habit of wearing lamp shades as hats don't photograph her in front of one! A plain background is best. Make sure that people in groups are roughly the same distance from the camera when you photograph them, otherwise the result is uneven exposure.

COMPETITION

GUIDES—Why don't you enter our photography competition and try and win a KODAK CAMERA OUTFIT? All you have to do is send us a photograph which you have taken yourself.

The competition is in three categories:

PEOPLE—a portrait of just one person, or a group

PLACES—perhaps a building you like, or an interesting view

ANIMALS—a photogenic pet, wild animals and birds, or farm animals

Entries can be in black and white or colour.
REMEMBER the points mentioned in SNAP HAPPY! and your photograph could be a winner. The sender of the best pictures in each category will win a KODAK CAMERA OUTFIT, donated by KODAK.
Please write your name, address, age and Guide Company on the back of each photograph, and send them in an envelope with a list of the three items you liked best in this annual, to THE EDITOR, PHOTOGRAPHY COMPETITION, THE GIRL GUIDE ANNUAL, 17-19 BUCKINGHAM PALACE ROAD, LONDON SW1W 0PT.
The closing date is March 31st 1983 and the winners will be notified by post. The editor's decision is final.

If you want your photograph returned you must enclose a stamped, addressed envelope.

THE VILLAGE HALL AFFAIR

by Ann Hillyer illustrated by Colin Shearing

"I don't think much of that new Guide, Heather, do you?" whispered Meryl to her friend Sue, as they joined the rest of their Patrol at the end of a particularly noisy meeting.

"Well, I've hardly spoken to her yet," replied Sue. "She doesn't go to our school, does she? I've seen her at the bus stop, waiting to go into town. Perhaps she goes to Highbury House."

"She can't do—not in that shabby mac," protested Meryl. "You know how strict Highbury are on uniform! No—I'll tell you something—I think she goes to Shillington!"

Sue gave a little gasp. Shillington was a large sprawling house, several miles out of town, for girls with special problems. Many of them had been in trouble with the police.

"I thought all Shillington girls were boarders," put in Lynn, their P.L.

"Some of them are allowed home to sleep," Meryl told her. "Anyway, I'm sure I'm right about Heather. She's got awful manners. I said hello in the Post Office the other day, when I was queueing behind her, and she didn't even answer. And look at her—see how she stares!"

The new Guide certainly did seem to stare. At that moment she had her eyes fixed on Skipper, who was asking for silence as she had an important message to announce.

"Just before you go," began the Guider in her clear voice, "I'm afraid I have some rather unpleasant news. You may remember that a few weeks ago, someone broke into this hall and damaged the light fittings. Then, last week, the drama group found that somebody had forced the lock on their props box and damaged the things inside. Well, this evening when I arrived I found the kitchen window had been broken and the sink was full of glass."

"But who did it?" "Why?" "Tell the police!" several girls cried.

"I've no idea who did it, and of course the police will be informed," answered the Guider, looking worried.

On their way home, Meryl and Sue discussed the village hall affair. As usual, Meryl had plenty to say. "I've a pretty good idea who might've had a hand in it," she began eagerly.

"Not your brother Sam and his gang?" asked Sue hesitantly. Meryl was always bragging about Sam's daring exploits.

"Of course not!" Meryl snapped. "Sam wouldn't get involved in anything nasty like that. No—I reckon it's Miss Bad-Mannered Heather and her Shillington friends!"

"You can't say that, Meryl," protested Sue. "Why, Heather's a Guide, the same as us. She wouldn't do anything like that! And we don't know for certain that she goes to Shillington."

"Don't we?" jeered Meryl. "Well, if she doesn't go to our school and she doesn't go to Highbury, where *does* she go? There aren't any other schools!"

Meryl stopped abruptly as Skipper came up behind them. She was talking to Heather.

"Night, Skipper! Night, Heather!" called Meryl as they passed. The Guider put up a hand to wave, but Heather appeared to be very engrossed in speaking to Skipper and did not reply.

"Hypocrite!" said Meryl fiercely. "Did you see her, hanging on to Skip's every word like that? Pretending to be so attentive and polite? Well, I'm sure I'm right about her. She can't pull the wool over *my* eyes!"

When Meryl arrived home, she heard a row going on in the sitting-room. The deep, angry tones of her father contrasted with the sharper voice of Sam.

"What's up, Mum?" asked Meryl.

"Don't go in there for a minute, Meryl, please," her mother begged. "Dad found Sam up at the rec with that gang of his, drinking cider and getting very silly."

The sitting-room door was thrown open and Sam rushed upstairs, looking white and shaken.

"I've warned Sam not to hang around with those louts again!" said Meryl's father sternly. "Let this be a warning to you, too, young lady—watch out who you make friends with!"

"Oh, yes, Dad," agreed Meryl. "There's this new girl at Guides—a really nasty piece of work. Rude and sly and really horrible. I wouldn't want *her* for a friend!"

The following week the Company had a shock when

they arrived at the village hall. Skipper was there with the Vicar, and both of them looked most distressed.

"I'm afraid we can't meet here tonight, girls," announced the Guider. "It seems that, directly after last week's meeting, somebody broke in and smashed up the cloakrooms. A team of workmen have been trying to get repairs done, but last night there was another break-in and some tools have gone missing. I must ask you—does anyone know anything about it?"

Meryl glanced across at Heather, whose eyes were wide and almost frightened-looking.

"She knows something!" hissed Meryl, nudging Sue's arm.

"The police are on their way," added the Vicar, "and we think young people are involved, because of the size of the footprints and so on. I'm very sorry about your meeting, girls, but I hope it won't be long before the intruders are caught!"

As the Guides drifted away, Meryl overheard Heather asking for a private word with the Guider.

"Perhaps she's going to own up!" suggested Meryl. "Perhaps she's scared now that the police are on her track. She's probably got a criminal record already!"

"Oh, Meryl!" cried Sue, exasperated. "Don't you think you're a bit unfair about Heather? After all—none of us really know her."

And to Meryl's indignation, Sue hurried off to walk home with Lynn.

Later that week, Meryl was shopping in the Post Office and heard a most interesting scrap of conversation. "So they've found out who did all that damage to the village hall," one woman was saying to another.

"Yes—and a good job, too! Did you hear about that new girl in the Guides—Heather somebody—lives in Woodland Close?"

"Yes—fancy, a young girl like that!"

Meryl felt like running all the way to Sue's to gloat over her news. Then she decided to wait. Let Sue find out for herself!

Heather was not at the next Guide meeting. "Left in disgrace, probably!" thought Meryl smugly, sitting down by Sue.

"I'm glad we are able to use the hall once again," began Skipper, looking round at the girls. "Now before we start our meeting, I want to say one or two things. The police have found that it was a gang of boys who caused the damage in this hall, and they are to be punished accordingly. It was Heather who discovered the culprits."

"Heather?" echoed Meryl.

"Yes," the Guider went on. "The boys were up at the rec, bragging about what they'd done and saying what they were going to do next time. They didn't think they'd be overheard, because at the time some men were there, cutting the grass with those mechanical grass-cutters."

"But I don't see how Heather could have overheard anything if those grass-cutters were working," put in Meryl. "They make such a din!"

"Ah—but you see, Heather is an expert lip-reader!" Skipper told her. "Didn't you know—she is almost completely deaf."

Meryl's jaw dropped, and Sue looked at her scornfully.

"Yes," continued Skipper, "that's why Heather goes to Oatlands—a special school for the deaf. She has had many operations on her ears, and as a matter of fact she has another one tomorrow. So that's why she's staying quietly at home this evening."

"But why didn't Heather tell us she was deaf?" persisted Meryl.

"She wanted to be accepted into the Company on an equal footing," explained Skipper. "No special favours or anything. I think she has proved herself an excellent Guide. If her operation is successful, she hopes to go to the same school as the rest of you. So I hope you'll give her the welcome she deserves!"

"It was that group of boys your brother used to hang around with," Sue told a crestfallen Meryl later on. "My mother told me. You're lucky Sam wasn't involved."

"Oh, Sue—I do feel mean about Heather," said Meryl.

"Well, so you should," replied Sue firmly. "You really didn't give her a chance, you know. I reckon she's got plenty of pluck, joining Guides and everything when she can't even hear!"

"You're right," agreed Meryl. "But I'm going to go round and see her, straight after the meeting, and tell her that she can expect some visitors in hospital—and a proper welcome into the Company when she comes back!"

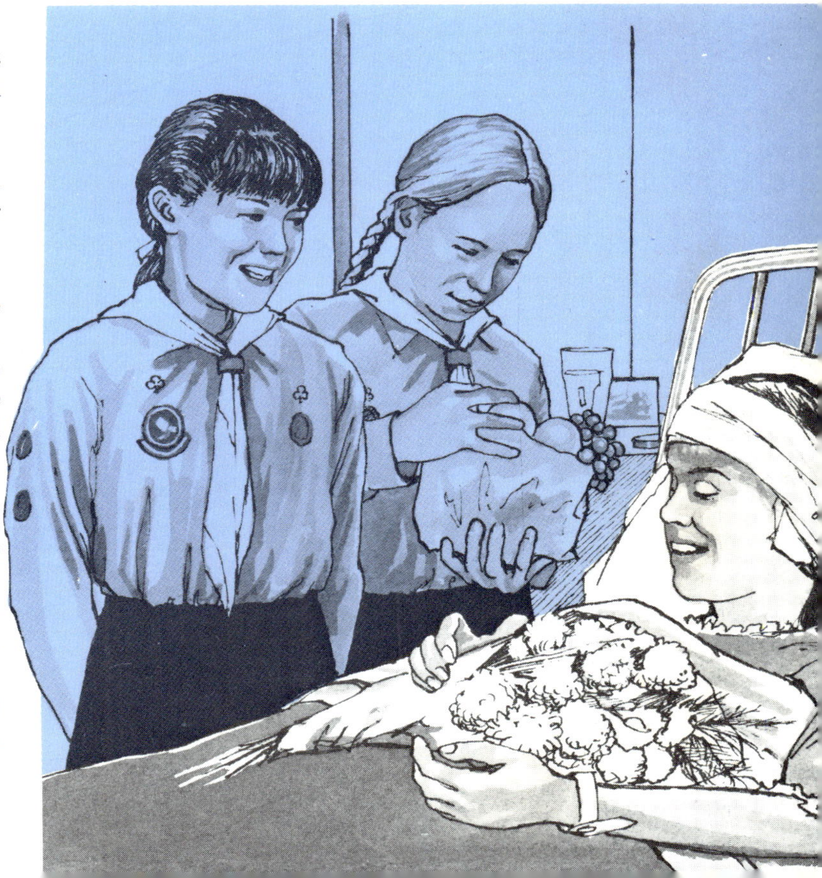

by William Dent

ANSWERS

GUIDING CROSSWORD

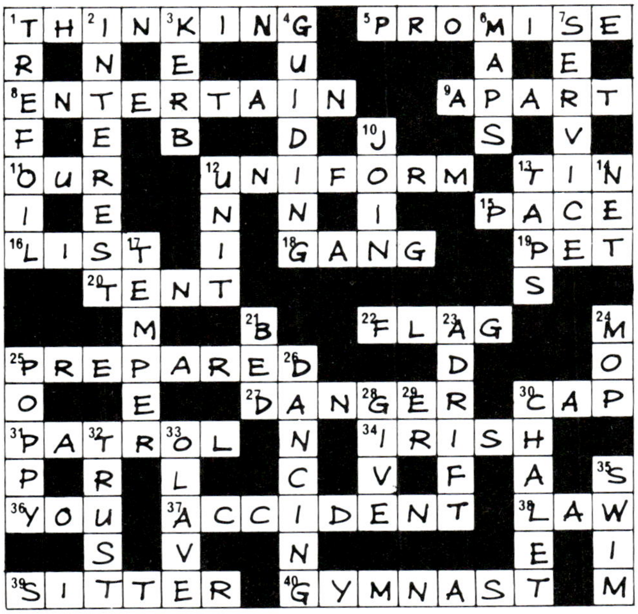

COOKERY DO!

1. Neither, there is no difference; 2. False. Keep them for about three days; 3. Could be any of these. To remedy, cut off the coating, blot the fish on soft kitchen paper, brush with butter, recoat with breadcrumbs and (fry, fry) fry again!; 4. Methylated spirit. Rub gently with a cloth starting from outside the stained area and working towards the centre; 5. c; 6. b and d; 7. Both—a and then b. Don't oil the top of the paper, though; 8. cockle—b, mussel—e, whelk—c, prawn—a, oyster—d; 9. b—use the lemon on white fish too, to keep it white and cut down cooking smells; 10. b, a, c; 11. Charles Dickens in *Nicholas Nickleby;* 12. Salads. Instead of using bottled salad cream, try mixing 2½ tbs of salad oil with salt, pepper, a pinch of dry mustard and 1 tbs malt or wine vinegar. There are many variations but these are the basic ingredients; 13. They will keep fresher if they are pointing downwards; 14. William Shakespeare in *Romeo and Juliet,* Act 4 Sc 2; 15. a) a steak of chopped and seasoned beef, fried; b) a well-seasoned German sausage, usually tinned in brine; c) a veal escalope dipped in breadcrumbs and fried in butter; d) a stew with liquid first made into a sauce; e) thyme, parsley and a bay leaf—or other herbs—tied in muslin, to flavour soups and stews; f) a mixture of wine or wine vinegar and oil in which meat is tenderised and flavoured before cooking; 16. George Meredith in *The Ordeal of Richard Feverel.*

FACE THE MUSIC

Prokofiev—Peter and the Wolf; Beethoven—Moonlight Sonata; Handel—Water Music; Schubert—Trout Quintet; Strauss—The Blue Danube.

GUIDE BADGE WORD SEARCH

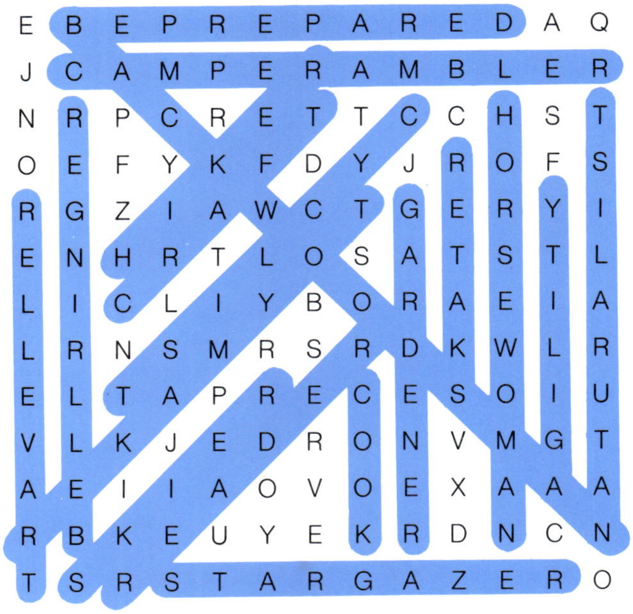

PATROL EMBLEMS

by Penny Morris

illustrated by Alexa Rutherford

When the Girl Guides first started, Patrols were only named after flowers, but before long girls asked to be allowed to choose other emblems. Trees and animals became popular, although nowadays most Patrols are named after birds and flowers. Here are a few of the more popular emblems. If your emblem doesn't have a motto, why not make one up based on the talents and strengths of your Patrol?

BLUEBELL—never give up hope

This flower is really the wild hyacinth, transforming the woods and hedgerows of Spring into a glorious carpet of hazy violet blue. The flower is bell-shaped for protection, so that rain will run down and off the flower without damaging the pollen within it. The mouth of the bell is wide enough to allow bees to enter and carry away pollen on their wings.

DAFFODIL—a merry heart maketh a cheerful countenance

Many poets have written of the delights of the cheerful daffodil. Legend says that the daffodil was originally white, and was worn by Persephone, the daughter of Ceres. When Pluto, god of the underworld, carried Persephone away, his sulphurous touch turned the flowers yellow. They fell to the ground, and a new yellow flower sprang up, the daffodil.

POPPY—dare to do right

This is one of our best known wild flowers, but it is greatly disliked by the farmer since its favourite site is the cornfield. Years ago people believed that if the petals fell when you picked a poppy, you were likely to be struck by lightning! It is a beautiful sight to see a field of nodding, flame red poppies.

RED ROSE—true patriots all

This is the flower of love and beauty. The rose originated in Persia, and it is not known how it spread to Europe, though Crusaders returning from Damascus brought roses to Northern France. Since then roses have spread throughout the world and they are now grown everywhere except arctic and equatorial regions.

SNOWDROP—hope for the best

The legend of the origin of this flower tells how Eve, banished from the garden of Eden, wept that she would never see the lovely garden again. An angel, taking pity on her, caught a snowflake as it fell. She breathed life into the snowflake and threw it down to Eve in the form of a snowdrop. Eve was so delighted by the little flower that the angel made a circle of them around her, dispelling her grief and filling her with hope.

THISTLE—smile and ignore the prickles of life

This plant, which is usually thought of as a weed, is the national emblem of Scotland, a magnificent purple colour. It was adopted by the Scots at the time of the Danish invasion of Scotland. The Danes crept up on the sleeping Scottish soldiers one night, and in the darkness one of the Danes put his bare foot on a thistle. His cry wakened the sleeping soldiers and they were able to defend their camp. The soldiers took the thistle as their emblem after this.